THE WORKERS' REVOLUTION
THE VIEW FROM

D0114973

4/16 - 5/2:

ALL

KAISER

THE WORKERS' REVOLUTION IN RUSSIA, 1917

THE VIEW FROM BELOW

Edited by
DANIEL H. KAISER
GRINNELL COLLEGE

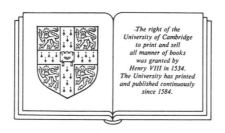

-The right of the
University of Cambridge
to print and sell
all manner of books
was granted by
Henry VIII in 1534.
The University has printed
and published continuously
since 1584.

CAMBRIDGE UNIVERSITY PRESS

CAMBRIDGE

NEW YORK   PORT CHESTER   MELBOURNE   SYDNEY

Published by the Press Syndicate of the University of Cambridge
The Pitt Building, Trumpington Street, Cambridge CB2 1RP
32 East 57th Street, New York, NY 10022, USA
10 Stamford Road, Oakleigh, Melbourne 3166, Australia

© Cambridge University Press 1987

First published 1987
Reprinted 1989

Printed in the United States of America

Library of Congress Cataloging-in-Publication Data
The Workers' revolution in Russia.
1. Soviet Union – History – Revolution, 1917–1921 –
Congresses.   2. Labor and laboring classes – Soviet
Union – Congresses.   3. Soviet Union – Social conditions –
1801–1917 – Congresses.   I. Kaiser, Daniel H., 1945–
DK265.A187   1987   947.084'1   87-9320

British Library Cataloguing in Publication Data
The Workers' revolution in Russia : the view
from below.
1. Soviet Union – History – Revolution,
1917–1921   2. Soviet Union – Politics
and government – 1917–1936
I. Kaiser, Daniel H.
947.084'1   DK265

ISBN 0 521 34166 3 hard covers
ISBN 0 521 34971 0 paperback

Contents

Preface

Long after the event, the Russian Revolution of 1917 remains poorly understood. The dominant view, enunciated by politicians and textbooks alike, holds that a small clique of activists somehow smuggled themselves into power in the Russian capital without the consent or assistance of the benighted masses. By sleight of hand and outside financing a cadre of loyalists managed to take over an empire and frustrate the desires of millions.

While agreeably tidy and remarkably clear, the dominant view of the Revolution conflicts with what we know to be the complex operation of human society. The revolutionary cadre that Lenin headed was certainly very motivated, but it seems doubtful that any group, however dedicated, could effect so sweeping a victory without at least the passive support of some elements of society. Present-day politics provides numerous examples of organized oppositions with substantial military and financial backing that are unable, nevertheless, to seize power. How is it that the Bolsheviks, only organized as a party about fifteen years before the Revolution and kept underground for much of that time, could so swiftly and easily snatch power?

In the course of teaching Russian history to undergraduates over the last decade, I found this implausible story more and more difficult to sustain. Not only did its simplicity not ring true, but Russia's own experience in the last years of the empire provided plenty of evidence for an alternative explanation. The extraordinary demands of rapid industrialization and extreme population growth that characterized tsarist society from about 1860 on put great pressure upon administrative and social bonds erected centuries earlier under entirely different circumstances. Russia's burgeoning industrial cities were forced to confront the symptoms of social stress: massive population migration, widespread strike activity, and in 1905 even revolution. A twentieth-century industrial order was emerging in the midst of a seventeenth-century agrarian society, and brought in its wake social disequilibrium and great turbulence. World War I exacerbated these difficulties, and simultaneously revealed the inability of tsarist government to cope with the situation. In other words, dramatic social change was itself enough to bring great shock waves to imperial Russian society, irrespective of the intentions of Russia's newly founded political parties.

Nevertheless, until recently it was difficult to provide students with the material to argue for a more complex understanding of the Russian Revolution. Memoirs of defeated politicians and the bombast of the victors dominated the materials in print. Over the last decade or so, the situation has changed. Now a few worker memoirs have appeared in English to complement the reminiscences of the political elite, and several excellent studies have established the connection between politics and society in revolutionary Russia. But these separate studies, addressed for the most part to scholarly audiences, were not easily accessible to the general reader or introductory student. Consequently, in the spring of 1984, with the support of the Grinnell College Rosenfield Program in Public Affairs, International Relations, and Human Rights, authors of four of these studies gathered at Grinnell College to talk about their work. The idea was not to introduce new research or talk to other specialists, but to synthesize their findings for a general audience and begin constructing an alternative explanation for the Russian Revolution.

The conference was so satisfying, both for the audience and the participants, that we decided to publish the papers so as to make readily available a general-audience introduction to the Russian Revolution. Authors of the original papers rewrote their essays after having discussed them at length during the conference and after having received written comments from the other participants. Two additional papers were commissioned to address aspects of the revolution that none of the original essays had developed. The authors received the revised essays of the other participants, and were invited to make their own contribution fit the purpose and context of the other papers. Consequently, each author attempted to bring a sense of the whole to his or her individual part. In my view, they have succeeded admirably.

Ronald Grigor Suny, Alex Manoogian Professor of Modern Armenian History at the University of Michigan, was among the first to direct attention to the intimate connections between politics and social change in the Russian Revolution with his book on the revolution in Baku. In the midst of his many other scholarly interests, Suny has continued to study the Revolution, and has also been particularly supportive of the most recent students of the Russian Revolution. In the present volume, he introduces the contrasting arguments, and points out how vital the social context is to understanding the Russian Revolution.

St. Petersburg was, as Russians have since often noted, the cradle of the revolution, and James H. Bater, Professor and Dean of the Faculty of Environmental Studies at the University of Waterloo, Ontario, knows revolutionary Petersburg very well. His study of St. Petersburg in the years of industrialization is an extremely informative illustration of the impact of political and economic decisions upon the mushrooming population of late imperial Russia. Author of numerous other studies on Russian social geography, Bater here surveys the St. Petersburg and Moscow environments to show just what pressures prerevolutionary Russian society was under.

How these pressures found expression in the factories of Petersburg is the subject of Steve A. Smith, lecturer in history at the University of Essex, Colchester, England. His book, *Red Petrograd: Revolution in the Factories, 1917–18*, takes the reader to the factory benches of the Russian capital where in many cases political and social radicalism far outdistanced the more modest aspirations of the professional politicians. Eschewing monolithic characterizations, Smith reveals the contrasting social composition of the factories and the resultant political differences. His essay explains exactly how the revolution felt in the factories and among the workforce for whom the Bolsheviks, Mensheviks, and Socialist Revolutionaries claimed to speak.

As Russians today still confirm, Moscow is very different from its sister city, the former St. Petersburg (now Leningrad). And in 1917 there were real differences in the history, social organization, and economic base of the two cities. But Diane P. Koenker, Associate Professor of History at the University of Illinois (Champaign-Urbana), points out that in many ways revolution-

ary Moscow was rather like St. Petersburg. By tracing worker
activism and union slogans, Koenker follows the evolution of
political attitudes among Moscow's working class, revealing at
one and the same time the similarities and contradictions in the
different layers of that society. Here again, the reader views political decisions from the perspective of the urban labor force.

Too often narrators of 1917 halt their story with the victory
of the Bolsheviks. But the October Revolution did not eradicate
all the tensions inherent in tsarist society, as William G. Rosenberg makes clear. Professor of History and Director of the Center for Russian and East European Studies at the University of
Michigan and a long-time student of the Russian Revolution,
Rosenberg in this text concentrates upon the relations between
the newly triumphant Bolsheviks and their erstwhile supporters
in the months after the October Revolution. As his essay makes
apparent, the general dissatisfaction with the political solutions
of early 1917 did not automatically translate into political satisfaction with the new Bolshevik government. Early in 1918 Petrograd's workforce found itself confronted with some very un-
pleasant consequences of Bolshevik policies; the result was friction,
helping to catapult the revolution into a very dark period.

Certainly no one book will be able to unravel all the complexities
that undergird so dramatic a social transformation as the Russian Revolution. Indeed, as William Rosenberg points out in the
conclusion here, there is much still to be learned. Already, an
entirely new generation of studies devoted to the revolution outside the capital cities points out just how unsatisfactory simplistic
explanations are. Everywhere there are exceptions and particular circumstances, and the contributors to the present book cannot claim to have finished the task.

But the essays presented here will help explain the Russian
Revolution not only from the viewpoint of cabinet minister or
expatriate general, but also from the perspective of metalworker
and textile factory employee. In the process, we hope to introduce a more comprehensive view of that most extraordinary event
in Russia's past.

DANIEL H. KAISER

Acknowledgments

The papers that form the core of this volume are the product of a symposium convened in February 1984 at Grinnell College. The college's Rosenfield Program in Public Affairs, International Relations, and Human Rights sponsored the symposium, and in that way supported the initial stage of this book. We are grateful to the Rosenfield Program and its former Director, Professor Joseph Frazier Wall. The college also provided support to prepare the volume for publication. Gladys Beaty, Karen Groves, and JoAnn Lauritzen cheerfully and efficiently entered the entire manuscript into a computer file.

Three of the papers included here derive from earlier, published versions. Ronald Suny's paper appeared in slightly different form under the title "Toward a Social History of the October Revolution," *American Historical Review* 88(1983):31–52, and is reprinted here with the permission of the American Historical Association. The contribution by James Bater borrows from two articles published earlier: "The Industrialization of Moscow and St. Petersburg" and "Modernization and the Municipality: Moscow and St. Petersburg on the Eve of the Great War," in *Studies in Russian Historical Geography,* James H. Bater and R. A. French, eds., 2 vols. (London: Academic Press, 1983), 2:279–327. Materials reprinted from those articles appear here with the permission of Academic Press. William Rosenberg's essay appeared in *Slavic Review* 44(1985):213–38 under the title "Russian Labor and Bolshevik Power after October," and is reprinted here by permission of the editor of *Slavic Review*. Most notes have been eliminated so as not to encumber the text. Those interested in fuller documentation may consult the original works.

Note on dates

Until February 1918 the Julian calendar, which in the twentieth century lagged behind the Gregorian calendar by thirteen days, prevailed in Russia. All dates in this volume are reported according to the calendar then in use in Russia.

1

Revising the old story: the 1917 revolution in light of new sources

Ronald Grigor Suny
University of Michigan

Issues of interpretation

Studying the Soviet Union is not quite like studying any other country in the world. While historians within the Soviet Union are compelled to portray their nation's past with the requisite degree of heroism and inexorable progress, in the West their colleagues face serious limitations of access to sources, the absence of basic works on aspects of Soviet history, and a variety of personal and political biases that inevitably influence the outcome of their research. Soviet historians write under the "guidance" of a political orthodoxy dictated by the party and colored in the language of Marxism-Leninism. Their Western counterparts attempt a cool objectivity, usually by dismissing the relevance of Marxism as an analytical tool and cloaking themselves in an ostensibly "value-free" social science. International rivalries, conflicting social values, and the more mundane exigencies of forging a professional career in a competitive marketplace determine the political and cultural contexts in which histories of the USSR are written. Nevertheless, many historians on both sides of the barricades seek freedom from bias, and in recent years more and more interesting work has appeared on Russia's history, both in the West and in the Soviet Union, which prompts a reconsideration of significant parts of that experience. After nearly seventy years of studying 1917, is it possible to come to some consensus on the contours and meaning of the 1917 Revolution?

1

2 *The workers' revolution in Russia, 1917*

The problem of the Russian Revolution is much more than an academic issue. The very question of the legitimacy or illegitimacy of the current Soviet government and its role in the world has been tied to the events of 1917. The eminent Harvard historian, Richard Pipes, has written:

> The elite that rules Soviet Russia lacks a legitimate claim to authority. ... Lenin, Trotsky, and their associates seized power by force, overthrowing an ineffective but democratic government. The government they founded, in other words, derives from a violent act carried out by a tiny minority. Furthermore, this power seizure was carried out under false pretenses. The coup d'état of October 1917 was accomplished not on behalf of the Bolshevik party but on behalf of the soviets. ... But although the Bolsheviks claimed to overthrow the Provisional Government in order to transfer power to these soviets, in reality they used them from the beginning as a façade behind which to consolidate their own authority, and the transfer was never accomplished.[1]

This statement, somewhat extreme in its formulation, nevertheless continues a tradition of historical interpretation that has seen the October seizure of power by the Bolsheviks as either a conspiratorial coup by a small band of adventurers with no real following, or as the result of a fortuitous series of accidents in the midst of the "galloping chaos" of the revolution. Either way the Bolshevik regime's beginnings are artificial and in no way organically linked to the real aspirations of the Russian people. These interpretations attribute Bolshevik success to the dominant and dynamic (sometimes demonic) personality of Lenin, a power-hungry genius who would stop at nothing to control Russia (and eventually the world). Various works have painted the most contradictory portraits of the founder of the Soviet state. Lenin has been portrayed both as sincere *and* as a "compulsive revolutionary," a gambler who understood that his small party had little to lose by risking everything on the October Revolution; at the same time some historians depict Lenin as the man most sensitive to the growing radicalization of the workers and soldiers who rode the wave of social discontent to an easy and nearly inevitable victory. In most cases the emphasis on Lenin (or on the efficient Bolshevik organization) as the key factor in Bolshevik victory has had the effect of downplaying the degree

[1] Richard Pipes, "Why the Russians Act Like Russians," *Air Force Magazine* (June 1970): 51–5, cited in Louis Menasche, "Demystifying the Russian Revolution," *Radical History Review* 18 (Fall 1978):153.

of support his party may have had among the lower classes and of contributing to the notion of the "illegitimacy" of the Soviet government.

Related to the political values brought to the study of the Soviet Union, and certainly connected to the overemphasis on personality and conspiracy in the history of the revolution, is a preference among many analysts of the USSR to concentrate on political, rather than more broadly social, explanations. In my view the entire history of revolutionary and postrevolutionary Russia has been interpreted to date too narrowly, with the result that political forms and ideas have been exaggerated as causative factors, and the underlying social and economic structures and conflicts in Russian society have been underplayed. The dominant model of interpretation of the Soviet system, the totalitarian model, is precisely this kind of theoretical construct that begins and ends with the political, with the all-encompassing power of the state, to the neglect of consideration of extrapolitical components of the system. For too long Russian history has been written not only from the top down, but with the bottom left out completely. Fortunately, in the last decade particularly, Western and Soviet historians have joined their European and American colleagues in other fields and introduced social historical approaches to the Russian field.

Rather than review in detail the arguments of the political historians versus the social historians, what I intend to do here is present an interpretation of the events of 1917 based on the work of recent social histories, and contrast their findings with the earlier interpretations. I am borrowing here, for reasons of economy and precision, from my own summary of this literature that appeared in the *American Historical Review*.[2]

Social polarization and the February revolution

The overthrow of the tsar, accomplished by workers and soldiers in Petrograd early in 1917, was the product of largely spontaneous action by thousands of hungry, angry, and war-weary

[2] Ronald Grigor Suny, "Toward a Social History of the October Revolution," *American Historical Review* 88(1983):31–52.

women and men who had lost confidence in the government of Nicholas II. But along with the political revolution aimed at autocracy, a deeply rooted social antagonism, particularly on the part of certain groups of workers, against the propertied classes (the so-called *tsenzovoe obshchestvo, census society*) was evident. This social cleavage was not simply a product of the years of war but predated that conflict, as Leopold H. Haimson has shown in his seminal articles published two decades ago.[3] Haimson argues that a dual polarization had been taking place in urban Russia in the last years before the war. As all but the most conservative strata of society moved away from the bureaucratic absolutist regime, the bottom of society, the working class – more precisely, workers in large firms such as the metalworks – was pulling away from the liberal intelligentsia, from moderates in the Social Democratic party, and from the Duma politicians. Writes Haimson,

By 1914 a dangerous process of polarization appeared to be taking place in Russia's major urban centers between an *obshchestvo* [society] that had now reabsorbed the vast majority of the once alienated elements of its intelligentsia (and which was even beginning to draw to itself many of the workers' own intelligentsia) and a growing discontented and disaffected mass of industrial workers, now left largely exposed to the pleas of an embittered revolutionary minority.[4]

In contrast to the usual picture of the Bolsheviks as an isolated clique among a generally economically oriented working mass, Haimson has demonstrated that a steady radicalization of the workers in the metal industry, and in Petersburg particularly, had resulted in a growth in Bolshevik influence at the expense of the Mensheviks and Socialist Revolutionaries. An increasing sense of class unity and separation from the rest of society combined with an awareness that workers themselves could take upon their shoulders the solution to their own problems. Ever more militant and far-reaching demands were put forth, most notably by Petersburg metalworkers, and the high incidence of defeat in their economic strikes only propelled them further toward a revolutionary opposition to the regime and the industrialists. "Given the even more precise correspondence between the image of the state and society that the Bolsheviks advanced and the instinctive

---

[3] Leopold H. Haimson, "The Problem of Social Stability in Urban Russia, 1905–1917," *Slavic Review* 23(1964):619–42; 24(1965):1–22.
[4] Ibid., 639.

outlook of the laboring masses, the Bolshevik party cadres were now able to play a significant catalytic role. They succeeded . . . in chasing the Menshevik 'Liquidators' out of the existing open labor organizations."[5] By 1914 the key labor unions were in the hands of the Bolsheviks, and working class discontent exploded in a sharp increase in the number and duration of strikes and political protests.

Although the war years demonstrated the fragility of the Bolsheviks' newly conquered positions within the working class and arrests and wartime patriotism ate into their influence, the potential for a renewal of militance remained intact. Much more visible than the exiled Bolshevik leaders were those more moderate socialists who remained in the capital and worked in the legal and semilegal institutions permitted by the autocracy. With the collapse of tsarism, timing and geography propelled even the less prominent Mensheviks and Socialist Revolutionaries into positions of enormous power and influence.[6] Although in the first month of revolution workers were neither unified around any one program nor tightly tied to any one party, there was a striking consensus among most Petrograd workers on the question of power, both in the state and the economy.[7] Except for the most militant workers, the metal workers of the Vyborg district, they were not yet anxious either to take state power or run the factories themselves. Thus there was a strategic parallel between their *conditional* support of the Provisional Government and the notion of "workers' control," which at this time meant merely the supervision of the owners' operations by representatives of the workers, not the organization of production directly by the workers.[8] Both the political and economic policies fa-

[5] Ibid., 638.
[6] For a detailed treatment of the revolutionary days of February–March, see Tsuyoshi Hasegawa, *The February Revolution: Petrograd 1917* (Seattle: University of Washington Press, 1981).
[7] On the question of party consciousness outside the capital, see Diane Koenker, "The Evolution of Party Consciousness in 1917: The Case of the Moscow Workers," *Soviet Studies* 30(1978):38–62.
[8] There has been debate on the exact meaning and dimensions of workers' control in 1917–18. See Chris Goodey, "Factory Committees and the Dictatorship of the Proletariat (1918)," *Critique* 3(1974):27–47; Maurice Brinton, "Factory Committees and the Dictatorship of the Proletariat," *Critique* 4(1975):78–86; Brinton, *The Bolsheviks and Workers' Control* (London: Solidarity, 1970); William G. Rosenberg, "Workers and Workers' Control in the Russian Revolution," *History Workshop* 5(Spring 1978):89–97; Rosenberg, "Workers' Control on the

vored by active workers in the first months of revolution entailed watching over and checking institutions that would continue to be run by members of propertied society.

Yet the social polarization of which Haimson has written was already evident even in the euphoria of February and early March, as the workers and soldiers set up their own class organizations – factory committees, soldiers' committees, their own militia, and most importantly, the soviets – to articulate and defend their interests.[9] From the beginning of the revolution they registered a degree of suspicion toward the Duma Committee and the Provisional Government, which were seen as the representatives of educated society. Among the rank-and-file soldiers the sense of distance and distrust toward their officers led them to form their own committees and draft the famous Order Number One that both legitimized the committees and placed the Petrograd garrison under the political authority of the soviet. Among the sailors of the Baltic Fleet, a force in which workers were much more heavily represented than in the peasant-based army, the hatred of the crewmen toward the officer elite resulted in an explosion of summary killings.[10] The sailors reflected the genuine suspicions of the lower classes who rejected any notion of a coalition government with the "bourgeoisie" and maintained that the soviet should remain a separate locus of power, critical of but not actively opposing the government. Thus Dual Power – the coexistence of two political authorities, the Provisional Government and the Soviet – was an accurate mirror of the real balance of forces in the city and the mutual suspicions that kept them from full cooperation.

Railroads," *Journal of Modern History* 49(1977):D1181–D1219; Carmen Sirianni, *Workers' Control and Socialist Democracy: The Soviet Experience* (London: Verso, 1982); and Steve A. Smith, *Red Petrograd: Revolution in the Factories, 1917–1918* (Cambridge: Cambridge University Press, 1983).

[9] Tsuyoshi Hasegawa, "The Formation of the Militia in the February Revolution: An Aspect of the Origins of Dual Power," *Slavic Review* 32(1973):303–22; "The Problem of Power in the February Revolution of 1917 in Russia," *Canadian Slavonic Papers* 14(1972):611–32; and "The Bolsheviks and the Formation of the Petrograd Soviet in the February Revolution," *Soviet Studies* 39(1977):86–107.

[10] Norman E. Saul, *Sailors in Revolt: The Russian Baltic Fleet in 1917* (Lawrence: The Regents Press of Kansas, 1978), 15–16. See also Evan Mawdsley, *The Russian Revolution and the Baltic Fleet: War and Politics, February 1917–April 1918* (London: Macmillan, 1978), 2–10.

The irony of the February Revolution was that the workers and soldiers had effectively overthrown the old government, but neither they nor their leaders were yet confident enough of their abilities to form their own government or prevent a counter-revolutionary challenge if they excluded the propertied classes. While they were reluctant to accept rule by their old class enemies, they realized that without agreement with the Temporary Duma Committee the loyalty of the army at the front was problematic.[11] The Duma leadership, on the other hand, understood that real power – the power to call people into the streets, defend the city, make things work or fall apart – was in the hands of the soviet, not the government. Both they and the moderate leaders were willing to play down the conflict within society in the face of a possible reaction from the right. The memory of 1905, when the army was used to reaffirm the power of the upper classes, was still vivid in many minds. Realism and caution through March and early April allowed a brief period of cooperation and conciliation that at first convinced many of the possibility of collaboration between the top and bottom of society, but ultimately created in its failure a bitter and divisive aftermath.

As early as March 10 the Soviet and the Petrograd Society of Factory and Works Owners came to an agreement to introduce an eight-hour working day in factories. This victory for the workers on an issue that had caused deep hostility in the prewar period was achieved with surprising ease, and the conciliatory attitude of industrialists like A. I. Konovalov seemed to predict further concessions. Employers also met demands for higher wages, and during the first three months of the revolution nominal wages rose on the average of fifty percent in Russia.[12] There was greater resistance to the idea of a minimum wage, but industrialists finally approved it too on April 24. Despite the fact that workers were trespassing on prerogatives traditionally held by capitalists when they demanded the removal of unpopular

[11] Allan K. Wildman, *The End of the Russian Imperial Army: The Old Army and the Soldiers' Revolt (March–April 1917)* (Princeton: Princeton University Press, 1980), 172.
[12] Ziva Galili y Garcia, "The Menshevik Revolutionary Defensists and the Workers in the Russian Revolution of 1917" (Ph.D. diss., Columbia University, 1979), chap. 2, p. 16.

administrative personnel, even some of these desires were satisfied.

As Ziva Galili y Garcia shows convincingly, even though there
was a significant decline in workers' suspicion toward the "bourgeoisie" in March, important groups among the industrialist class
now expressed their opposition to the "excessive demands" of
the workers.[13] Even Konovalov, an advocate of cooperation with
the workers and the Minister of Trade and Industry in the Provisional Government, held that the overthrow of tsarism should
rightly result in the establishment of the commercial–industrial
bourgeoisie as the dominant force in Russia's social and economic life. Although this notion seems superficially to agree with
the Menshevik conception of the revolution as "bourgeois–
democratic," there were serious tactical differences between
middle-class leaders like Konovalov and the Menshevik Revolutionary Defensists on the left. Whereas the first Congress of
Trade and Industry called for restoration of "free trade" and
the placing of food supply in the hands of the "experienced
commercial–industrial class," Menshevik economists favored price
regulation and state control of the economy. But the issue that
brought down the fragile Dual Power arrangement was not the
emerging economic issue but the conflict between the upper and
lower classes on the war.

Initially the soldiers were suspicious of Dual Power and even
of the Soviet to some extent, but Allan K. Wildman demonstrates that soldiers began to perceive the Provisional Government as a "class" rather than a "national" institution.[14] One by
one, the soldiers' congresses held at the various fronts came out
in support of soviet control over the government and for a
"democratic peace without annexations or contributions." In April
soldiers and workers poured into the streets to protest the government's continued support for the war aims of the deposed
tsarist regime. The April crisis marked the end of the futile attempt by Minister of Foreign Affairs P. N. Miliukov and his closest associates to maintain a foreign policy independent of the
Soviet. The same cleavage that was visible in Petrograd between
the lower classes and propertied society on questions of power,

[13] Ibid., 27.   [14] Wildman, *End of the Russian Imperial Army*, 320.

economy, and the war was also reflected within the army between the soldiers and their officers.

The dependence of the Provisional Government on the Soviet, clear from the first days of their coexistence, required in
the view of the members of the government the formation of a
coalition. At first resistant to joining a government of the bourgeoisie, the Mensheviks reluctantly agreed in order to bolster
the government's authority. For I. G. Tsereteli, the most influential Menshevik who joined the government, coalition meant
the unification of the workers with other "vital forces of the nation" in an effort to end the war and fight social disintegration.
As Galili y Garcia points out, the successful collaboration between the bourgeoisie and the Soviet in the first months of the
revolution had lulled the Mensheviks into believing that class
hostility could be overcome. But just as the coalition was being
formed, the economic situation grew worse. Inflation forced more
demands for wages, but industrialists who had recently been so
cooperative now were resistant to further raises. In May and June
workers began to suspect that factory shutdowns were deliberate
attempts at sabotage by the owners. Economic difficulties, so in-
timately tied to the war, turned workers against the industrialists
and the government.[15] Though some workers supported coalition, the great bulk of Petrograd's factory workers grew increasingly suspicious, both of the government and of those socialists
who collaborated with the bourgeoisie. The beneficiary of this
suspicion and disgust was the party that opposed the coalition
and advocated a government made up of the representatives of
the working people – the Bolsheviks.[16]

The association of the Menshevik and Socialist Revolutionary
(SR) leaders of the Soviet with the coalition government, and
consequently with the renewed war effort in June, placed a stark

---

[15] Galili y Garcia, "Menshevik Revolutionary Defensists," chap. 6, pp. 3–17.
[16] The predominant Western image of the Bolshevik Party as a party of *intelligenty* divorced from the working class has been challenged by quantitative studies
by William Chase and J. Arch Getty on the Moscow Bolsheviks. They have
concluded that the party, while "primarily composed of and dominated by
intelligenty" up to 1905, "so radically altered its social composition [after 1905]
that, by 1917, the Bolsheviks could honestly claim to represent a large section
of the working population." Chase and Getty, "The Moscow Bolshevik Cadres
of 1917: A Prosopographic Analysis," *Russian History* 5, pt. 1 (1978):95.

choice before the workers and soldiers: either cooperation and collaboration with the upper classes, who were increasingly perceived as enemies of the revolution, or going it alone in an all-socialist soviet government. The first efforts of the lower classes were directed at convincing the Soviet leaders of the need to take power into their own hands. The erosion of lower-class support for the government was already quite clear on May 31 when the workers' section of the Petrograd Soviet voted for the Bolshevik resolution calling for "All Power to the Soviets!" Even more dramatic was the demonstration of June 18 in which hundreds of thousands of workers marched carrying slogans such as "Down with the Ten Capitalist Ministers!" By early July, with the distressing news of the failure of the June offensive filtering into the city, the more militant soldiers, sailors, and workers attempted through an armed rising to force the Soviet to take power. Emblematic of the paradox of the situation is the famous scene when sailors surrounded V. M. Chernov, SR Minister of Agriculture in the coalition government, and yelled at him: "Take power, you son-of-a-bitch, when it is given to you."[17]

Radicalization of the workers

But, as is well known, the Soviet did not take power, and a series of weak coalition governments followed the July crisis until their forcible overthrow in October. The rise of the Bolsheviks from isolation and persecution in July to state power in October has been the object of enormous historical study, but in the search for an explanation historians have tended to overemphasize the role of political actors, like Lenin and Trotsky, and to underestimate the independent activity of workers and soldiers. More recently, the workers have returned to center stage. Diane Koenker, Steve Smith, David Mandel, and others, have investigated the process that radicalized the workers. Their research suggests that the workers came to feel that the Provisional Government, even in its coalition variant, was not particularly re-

[17] Alexander Rabinowitch, *Prelude to Revolution: The Petrograd Bolsheviks and the July 1917 Uprising* (Bloomington: Indiana University Press, 1968), 188. The source for this scene is P. N. Miliukov, *Istoriia vtoroi russkoi revoliutsii*, vol. 1 (Sofia, 1921), 244.

sponsive to worker needs, and that factory owners were hostile
to the gains made by workers in the February Revolution. Workers' frustration with the hostile middle and upper classes was
both a revival of prewar attitudes of the most militant workers
and a reaction to perceived counterrevolutionary attitudes and
actions of industrialists, intellectuals (both liberal and socialist),
and, in time, the government.

Historians who have looked most closely at workers' activities
have replaced the superficial impression of chaos and anarchy
with a view that describes workers' actions in 1917 as a "cautious
and painful development of consciousness," part of "an essentially rational process."[18] The contours of worker activity are
complex, but not chaotic. One analyst of Petrograd labor, David
Mandel, distinguishes three principal strata of workers – the politically aware skilled workers (primarily the metalworkers of the
Vyborg district), the unskilled workers (largely women textile
workers), and the "worker aristocracy" (characterized best by the
pro-Menshevik printers). Mandel shows that the metalworkers
were most radical in the political sphere, calling for the early
establishment of soviet power, while the unskilled workers, who
tended to be more moderate in political questions, exhibited the
greatest militancy in the wage struggle.[19] Steve Smith breaks down
the metalworkers into shops and carefully delineates between
"hot" shops, such as foundries, where newly arrived peasant-
workers could be found, and "cold" shops, such as machine shops,
where the highly skilled and literate workers proved to be most
receptive to Social Democratic activists.[20] Looking at the Putilov
works, Smith notes that in this giant enterprise workers moved
more slowly toward the Bolsheviks than in other metalworking
plants and that "shopism" (loyalty to and identification with one's

---

[18] David Mandel, *The Petrograd Workers and the Fall of the Old Regime: From the
February Revolution to the July Days, 1917* (London: Macmillan, 1983), 3.

[19] Ibid., chap. 3; David Mandel, *Petrograd Workers and the Soviet Seizure of Power
(July 1917–June 1918)* (London: Macmillan, 1984), 246–7.

[20] Steve A. Smith, "Craft Consciousness, Class Consciousness: Petrograd 1917,"
History Workshop 11(Spring 1981):36. The central argument of Smith's article
coincides with Mandel's view of growing worker militancy and class consciousness. He points out that "shopism" and "factory patriotism" did not preclude
labor militancy or inhibit "the development of a broader sense of belonging to
a class of working people whose interests were antagonistic to those of the
employers" (p. 51).

place of work, rather than the class of workers as a whole) and conciliationism remained stronger here than elsewhere.[21]

Two recent studies of factory committees in the Russian Revolution, by Carmen Sirianni and Steve Smith, significantly revise the generally accepted view of the activities of these committees.[22] Formerly scholars and other writers had argued that the plant-level organizations of workers were marked by a decentralized, anarcho-syndicalist approach to economic activity, that they were in large part responsible for the decline in productivity during the revolution and civil war, and that they contributed far more to the chaos of the revolution than to any solution of the economic collapse. Smith and Sirianni persuasively demonstrate that the committees were far more interested in keeping the factories running than had previously been assumed, and that much of their activity was directed at preventing what they considered to be "sabotage." When owners tried to maintain their own authority in factories and sometimes resorted to abandoning the factory or closing it down, workers' committees attempted to keep factories running, even in the absence of owners and without the cooperation of white-collar workers, engineers, and technicians.

Rather than some visceral hostility to the bosses or an anarchist appetite for overturning authority, the actual practice of factory committees was to restructure the organization of the factory regime more democratically. This might involve the expulsion of particularly hated foremen or police spies. It might also mean the institution of "workers' control," usually the supervision by workers' committees of the activities of the bosses and managers who still ran the plant. In extreme cases, particularly after the October Revolution, it might mean the complete takeover of an enterprise by the workers. But as Smith shows most conclusively, these "nationalizations from below" were almost invariably defensive and designed only to keep the factories running. Russian workers were as interested (perhaps even more interested) as any other social class in keeping the plants running as well as possible. As the economic situation worsened in the summer of 1917, workers' suspicion of the upper levels of society was translated into struggles for greater control within

---

[21] Ibid., 37.   [22] Sirianni, *Workers Control;* Smith, *Red Petrograd.*

the factories and increased opposition to those moderate socialists who backed the coalition government.

Although the rapidity of labor radicalization in Petrograd is
certainly distinctive, similar processes, marked by growing class
cohesion and consciousness, were evident in other parts of the
country, as my own work on Baku and Donald Raleigh's on Saratov demonstrate.[23] By engaging in a detailed and quantitative
study of the dynamics of labor activity in Moscow, Diane Koenker
has also concluded that:

one must . . . reject the image of the Russian working class as uniformly
irrational, poorly educated, and incapable of independent participation
in the political process. One must reject in particular the myth that the
revolution in the cities was carried out by dark semi-peasant masses
"who did not understand the real meaning of the slogans they loudly
repeated." Yes, of course, many Moscow workers were more rural than
urban; but when one looks at the participation levels of different segments of the urban labor force, the fact that skilled urban cadres, not
the unskilled peasant mass, were the leading political actors can be seen
over and over again. These workers possessed experience, political connections, and the degree of economic security which enabled them to
function freely and easily in the political life of 1917.[24]

The radicalization of workers in the first year of the revolution was an "incremental process, which took place in response
to specific economic and political pressures."[25] Other studies bear
out the same conclusion. When Galili y Garcia explains the delayed radicalization of the less politically conscious unskilled
workers in the second quarter of 1917, she observes that these
less well organized workers had not benefited from the initial
round of wage raises in March and April. By the time they made
their bid for higher pay, the industrialists had adopted a more
intransigent attitude.[26] By mid-May the number of unemployed
workers in Petrograd and other industrial cities was rising con-
spicuously, and as real wages continued to plummet and mass
dismissals accelerated, more and more less-skilled workers joined

---

[23] See the chapter, "From Economics to Politics," in Ronald Grigor Suny, *The
Baku Commune, 1917–1918: Class and Nationality in the Russian Revolution*
(Princeton: Princeton University Press, 1972), 102–46. Donald J. Raleigh,
Revolution on the Volga: 1917 in Saratov (Ithaca: Cornell University Press, 1985).
[24] Diane Koenker, *Moscow Workers and the 1917 Revolution* (Princeton: Princeton
University Press, 1981), 360.
[25] Ibid., 363–4.
[26] Galili y Garcia, "Menshevik Revolutionary Defensists," chap. 5, pp. 43–62.

the "proletarians" in a commitment to soviet power. By June –
July a majority of Petrograd workers were already opposed to
the coalition government and shared a sense of separate and
antagonistic interests between workers and the propertied classes.
A greatly heightened sense of class was apparent among the mass
of workers by the summer.

The studies of Mandel, Galili y Garcia, Koenker, Smith, and
others provide the reader with the specifics of the economic and
political stimuli that led to radicalization; for the first time it is
possible to understand how individual grievances within the larger
context of social polarization combined to create class antagonisms. Given that Russia's workers had long been closely involved with a radical socialist intelligentsia anxious to forge a
Marxist political culture within the urban labor force, it is hardly
surprising that workers in 1917 should "naturally" come to a
"class-oriented viewpoint." Koenker sums up this development
in her conclusion, that gives us social history with the politics left
in:

> That the revolutionary unity of March fell apart along class lines can be
> attributed to economic conditions in Russia, but also to the fact that the
> class framework was after all implicit in socialist consciousness. Capital-
> ists began to behave as Marx said they would: no concessions to the
> workers, no compromise on the rights of factory owners. Mensheviks
> and SRs tried to straddle both sides of the class split; this appeal can be
> seen in the mixed social composition of their supporters. The Bolshe-
> viks, however, had offered the most consistent class interpretation of
> the revolution, and by late summer their interpretation appeared more
> and more to correspond to reality. . . . By October, the soviets of work-
> ers' deputies, as the workers' only class organ, seemed to class-conscious
> workers to be the only government they could trust to represent their
> interests.[27]

While workers increasingly perceived common interests with
their fellow workers and shared antagonisms toward the rest of
society, the upper levels of society too felt a growing hostility
toward the lower classes. William G. Rosenberg has illustrated
this shift to the right by the Kadets as the liberals' growing identification with commercial and industrial circles changed them
from a party of liberal professionals and intellectuals into Rus-

---

[27] Koenker, *Moscow Workers*, 364.

sia's party of the bourgeoisie.[28] Even as they persisted in maintaining their "no-class" ideology, the Kadets emerged as the de facto defenders of a capitalist order and the determined opponents of the approaching social revolution desired by the more militant of the lower classes. Isolation from the socialist workers and soldiers led the liberals to turn to the military as a source of order and power. Rosenberg argues, as had the Left Kadets in 1917, that the only hope for a democratic political outcome in Russia was lost when the Kadets failed to work effectively with the moderate socialists in the coalition government and make significant concessions to the lower classes. "The very coalition with moderate socialists that Miliukov and the new tacticians strove for so persistently in emigration [after the Civil War] *was* possible in the summer of 1917."[29] The failure to form such a liberal–socialist alternative to Bolshevism might be seen as the consequence of the Kadets' lack of "true liberal statesmanship," but Rosenberg's analysis permits us to develop an alternative interpretation.[30] With the Kadets evolving into the principal spokesmen of propertied Russia, it was increasingly unlikely that they would compromise the interests of the privileged classes that backed them in order to form a dubious alliance with the lower orders whose ever more radical demands threatened the very existence of privilege and property. The Kadets' claim to stand above class considerations was simply a utopian stance in a Russia that was pulling apart along class lines.

To underestimate the extent of the social polarization and the perceived irreconcilability of the interests of the lower classes and propertied society within the constraints of the February regime would lead one away from a satisfactory explanation of the victory of the Bolsheviks and toward a reliance on accidental factors of will and personality. Only through a synthesis of political and social history, in which the activity and developing polit-

---

[28] William G. Rosenberg, *Liberals in the Russian Revolution: The Constitutional Democratic Party, 1917–1921* (Princeton: Princeton University Press, 1974), 31, 154–5.

[29] Ibid., 469.

[30] For a fuller exposition of my pessimism concerning a liberal–moderate socialist coalition in 1917, see Suny, "Some Thoughts on 1917: In Lieu of a Review of William Rosenberg's *Liberals in the Russian Revolution*," *Sbornik: Papers of the First Conference of the Study Group on the Russian Revolution* (Leeds, 1975), 24–7.

ical consciousness of workers, soldiers, and sailors is taken seriously, can the Bolshevik victory be adequately explained.

Society and government

Against the background of deepening social cleavage with all its incumbent aspects of fear and suspicion, hope and despair, the question of power was posed in the summer and fall of 1917. By the summer of 1917 there were four possible solutions to the problem of who would rule Russia. Tsereteli, Kerensky, the Menshevik Revolutionary Defensists, and the Right Socialist Revolutionaries advocated the first solution: a continuation of the coalition government, a policy of social unity and class collaboration to defend Russia against its external enemies and to prevent civil war. But such a solution was doomed in the face of the deepening social crisis and political paralysis. Given the hostility between classes and the mutually antagonistic aspirations and interests, a coalition government could move neither to the Left nor to the Right without stirring up opposition. It could neither satisfy the demands of the peasants for land nor attempt to protect the landlords' rights to private property. Paralyzed between its competing constituencies, all movement looked like vacillation, the product of a lack of will or determination, but in fact was the result of the real political bind faced by a government stretched between the extremes of a splintering society.

A second solution was a government made up of the upper classes alone, that is, a dictatorship of the Center and the Right. The Kadet leader, Miliukov, had desired such a government at the beginning of the revolution, but it proved to have no base of support in the population and collapsed finally in the April crisis. Real power was in the hands of the Soviet, and as the liberal Stankevich quipped: "The Soviet could make the Provisional Government resign with a telephone call."[31] The only possible way for the upper classes to rule – and the liberals as well as the Right came to this conclusion by summer – was to establish a military dictatorship. Kerensky and Kornilov made such an at-

[31] As quoted in David S. Anin, "The February Revolution: Was the Collapse Inevitable?" *Soviet Studies* 18(1967):448.

tempt in August, but disagreements over the final disposition of power and the actions of workers, soldiers, and soviets combined to thwart Kornilov. With the failure of the military coup d'état, the only possibilities left were for governments by one or several of the Soviet parties.

The third solution, and the one probably most desired by the lower classes in urban Russia, was an all-socialist government representing the workers, soldiers, and peasants of Russia, but excluding propertied society. A broader variant of this solution would have included nonsoviet "democratic" elements, such as municipal and government workers, people from cooperatives, and small shopkeepers. Historians seem to agree that when workers and soldiers voted for soviet power, they were in fact opting for a multiparty government of the leftist parties. This solution was never really implemented because of the serious divisions between the moderate socialists and the Bolsheviks, and there is legitimate doubt that the former defenders of coalition and the advocates of working-class rule could have lasted long in an all-socialist coalition.

In October 1917 the Bolsheviks came to power in the name of the Soviet. The coalition government had been completely discredited, and almost no one would defend it in its last hours. The Military Revolutionary Committee merely completed the process of political conquest of the Petrograd population that the Bolsheviks had started months earlier.[32] Bolshevik policy, alone of the political programs, corresponded to and reflected the aspirations and perceived interests of workers, soldiers, and sailors in Petrograd. Even without much direct participation in the October Days, the workers acquiesced in and backed the seizure of power by the Soviet. Lenin and a few others had seen

[32] Soviet historians estimate that the actual balance of forces in Petrograd on the eve of the insurrection involved about three hundred thousand armed supporters of the Bolsheviks and only about twenty-five thousand ready to fight for the Provisional Government. At the storming of the Winter Palace, the Bolshevik Red Guards, soldiers, and sailors numbered approximately twenty thousand with defenders of the palace estimated at about three thousand. In the fighting from October 24 to October 26, fewer than fifteen people were killed and fewer than sixty wounded. Roy A. Medvedev, *The October Revolution*, trans. George Saunders (New York: Columbia University Press, 1979); Medvedev bases his figures on E. F. Erykalov, *Oktiabr'skoe vooruzhennoe vosstanie v Petrograde* (Leningrad, 1966), 303–4, 434–5, 461, 462.

the potential in 1917 for a government of the lower classes. He, earliest of almost all political leaders, had understood that in this revolution, marked by deep, long-standing social tensions and stoked by a seemingly endless war, unification of "all the vital forces of the nation" became increasingly unlikely. By late spring an all-class or nonclass government was no longer possible, and by linking his party's fortunes to the real social movement in Petrograd, Lenin was able to destroy the flimsy coalition of liberals and moderate socialists and effect a seizure of power in the name of the Soviet.

But instead of soviet power or socialist democracy, the Russian people eventually received a dictatorship of the Bolshevik Party. This was the fourth possible solution to the question of power. Why it succeeded over the more democratic third solution is a question that goes beyond the limits of this review, for the answer lies not so much in 1917 as in the long years of Civil War. Again, the answer to this question cannot be provided by resorting to personal and ideological influences, or by extending the analysis based on politics alone, but rather through an examination of the intense class struggle that was carried beyond the limits of the city of Petrograd into the countryside and all the provinces of Russia.

A new paradigm

As historians have shifted their attention away from the political elites to the people in the streets, the victorious Bolsheviks have appeared less to be Machiavellian manipulators or willful conspirators than alert politicians with an acute sensitivity to popular moods and desires. Without forgetting the authoritarian traits in Lenin, Trotsky, and other Bolshevik leaders or the power of the image of the party outlined in *What Is To Be Done?*, we can move on to a new paradigm for understanding 1917 that reduces the former reliance on party organization or personal political skills so central to older explanations.

 The key to a new paradigm is an appreciation of the deepening social polarization that drew the upper and middle classes together and away from the workers, soldiers, and peasants. Propertied society, after an initial period of compromise in the

early spring of 1917, began to resist encroachments on its prerogatives in the economy and in foreign policy and, faced by
growing militance of the workers and soldiers, developed a clearer
and more coherent sense of its own political interests. Likewise,
the workers and soldiers, confronted by lockouts, falling wages,
a renewal of the war effort, and perceived sabotage of the revolution, evolved their own sense of class interests. In time both
parts of Russian society found their interests to be incompatible,
and those parties that tried to stand "above class" or to unite "all
the vital forces of the nation" found themselves either forced to
take sides with one major force or abandoned by their former
supporters.

For Russians in 1917 the revolution was a struggle between
classes in the inclusive sense of the *verkhi* (upper classes) versus
the *nizy* (lower classes). Those broad antagonistic "classes" coalesced in the course of 1917. The heightened feeling of class was
forged in the actual experience of 1917 and contained both social hostilities bred over many years and intensified under wartime and revolutionary conditions, and a new political understanding that perceived soviet government as a preferable
alternative to sharing power with the discredited upper classes.
The Bolsheviks had since April advocated a government by the
lower classes, and with the failure of the coalition and its socialist
supporters to deliver on the promise of the revolution, the party
of Lenin and Trotsky took power with little resistance and the
acquiescence of the majority of the people of Petrograd. The
Bolsheviks came to power, not because they were superior manipulators or cynical opportunists, but because their policies, as
formulated by Lenin in April and shaped by the events of the
following months, placed them at the head of a genuinely popular movement. Sadly for those who had overthrown autocracy
and turned to the Bolsheviks to end the war and alleviate hunger, that solution based on a soviet government evolved inexor-
ably through a ferocious civil war into a new and unforeseen
authoritarianism.

2

St. Petersburg and Moscow on the eve of revolution

James H. Bater
University of Waterloo, Ontario

St. Petersburg, or Petrograd as it was named in deference to anti-German sentiment after the outbreak of world war in August 1914, was the main theater of revolutionary activity. But it was by no means the only one. Moscow and numerous other Russian cities figured prominently in the events that brought down the old order. In the final decades of late imperial Russia the changes associated with modernization profoundly altered the Russian city and transformed the conditions of daily life and labor for most of its inhabitants. Urban industrialization obviously played an important role in this general process of social, economic, and, ultimately, political change. In few places were the consequences more plainly to be seen than in the Empire's principal cities, Moscow and St. Petersburg, which are the focus of attention in this chapter. My purpose is to describe some features of the urban environment that might serve as a backdrop to the revolution of 1917. Before embarking on this task, however, it is necessary to sketch in broad outline the pattern of

Much of this chapter is drawn from my earlier writings, primarily: James H. Bater, *St. Petersburg: Industrialization and Change* (London: Edward Arnold, 1976); "Some Dimensions of Urbanization and the Response of Municipal Government: Moscow and St. Petersburg," *Russian History* 5, pt. 1 (1978): 46–63; "The Industrialization of Moscow and St. Petersburg" and "Modernization and the Municipality: Moscow and St. Petersburg on the Eve of the Great War," in *Studies in Russian Historical Geography*, eds. James H. Bater and R. A. French, 2 vols. (London: Academic Press, 1983), 2:279–303, 305–27; "Modernization and Public Health in St. Petersburg, 1890–1914," *Forschungen zur Osteuropaischen Geschichte* 37(1985):357–72.

population growth and industrial development in the Empire as a whole.

Citizens and cities in late imperial Russia

During the nineteenth century Russia grew significantly both in areal extent and in number of subjects. In the first quarter of the century the Caucasus region with its predominantly Christian, but ethnically diverse and non-Slavic peoples, was brought into the ambit of Empire. The process of territorial expansion continued throughout the second half of the century as Moslem Middle Asia and the formerly Chinese southern flank of the Russian maritime Far East region were acquired. The Russo–Japanese War of 1904–5 put an end to further Russian expansionism, and indeed resulted in a loss of some eastern territories. Over the century the process of territorial acquisition added substantially to the number of Russian citizens.

In 1810 the admittedly rudimentary means of enumerating the Empire's subjects put the total at around 41 million; in 1860 at 74 million. According to the only scientific census of the Empire's population there were nearly 125 million in 1897, including the Grand Duchies of Warsaw and Finland. By 1914 there were an estimated 160 million people living within Russian borders. The population was huge, but so too was the areal extent of the Empire. Few regions had high population densities, and nowhere was the population heavily concentrated in cities. Imperial Russia remained predominantly rural to the end. So too did its subjects remain largely illiterate and, owing to the high birth rate, demographically young.

Insofar as the data on demographic trends are accurate, they indicate that from the mid-nineteenth century to the end of the imperial era, birth rates and death rates both declined. In 1860 the birth rate was a shade more than 50 per 1,000 population. The death rate stood at about 37 per 1,000, and therefore the crude rate of net natural increase per 1,000 was 13. Improvements in public health and sanitation, especially during the final decades of the era, produced a more rapid decline in the death rate than occurred in the birth rate. By 1913 the crude rate of net natural increase per 1,000 population had risen to nearly 17.

Given the huge absolute size of the Empire's population, this translated into an annual increase of more than 2.5 million. Although public health improvements figured in the higher crude rate of net natural increase, most objective measures of public health and welfare in Russia indicated that it still fared poorly in comparison with its industrializing European counterparts. The number of medical personnel is a case in point.

In 1889, for instance, there were just over 12,500 medical doctors in the whole of Russia, a ratio of 8.4 doctors for every 100,000 inhabitants. In the latter half of the 1880s the ratios of doctors per 100,000 population in Germany, England, France, and Austria were 30.9, 63.8, 31.1, and 20.8, respectively. Although ensuring reasonable standards of public health in Russian cities was often compromised owing to hypercongestion and inadequate basic municipal services, urban Russia could at least boast of having the largest share of medical doctors in the Empire. In the capital, St. Petersburg, there were around 1,500 doctors, a third more than in Moscow. This worked out to be a ratio of roughly 150 doctors for every 100,000 people. But in neither St. Petersburg nor in Moscow could public health matters be said to be of an especially high order. Meanwhile, in the Russian countryside there was one doctor serving the needs, on average, of 33,000 inhabitants.

In light of such statistics it should come as no great surprise to learn that life expectancies in the late imperial era were short. In 1887, for instance, the average life expectancy of the population of European Russia was just thirty-two years. High rates of infant mortality, and a harsh life for many of those who did survive to adulthood, were major contributing factors. A substantial number of peasants showed the physical manifestations of an impoverished existence. For example, between 1899 and 1901 fully one-fifth of the military conscripts called up were rejected as physically unfit. Peasant impoverishment was in no sense universal, however. In some regions regular, bountiful harvests played a part in the emergence of a prosperous class of peasant farmers, most notably after the Stolypin Agrarian Reforms of 1906–10. But generally speaking, the physical conditions for agriculture in Russia were more often begrudging than beneficent. The resultant variable annual harvest, combined with an inadequate internal transport system and increasingly economically stratified peasantry, frequently resulted in local famines, despite net exports of grain from the Empire as a whole. Thus, across rural Russia there were marked regional variations in the annual crude rate of net natural increase. Those who lived in the cities did not fare better, in a demographic sense, than those who lived in the villages. Indeed, throughout much of urban Russia the death rate frequently exceeded the birth rate until late in the nineteenth century. Any urban growth was being fed by in-migration from the countryside. Improvements in public health and sanitation, and a growing trend toward more female migrants and a more permanent attachment to the city, thereby enhancing the rate of family formation, eventually produced a demographic transition.

Russia's urban population was always small in relative terms. At mid-nineteenth century about 3.4 million people were officially classified as urban, barely 5 percent of the total population. By 1914 there were more than 28 million people living in urban places, but this was still less than one-fifth of the total population. In England, France, Germany, and the United States, for instance, urbanites comprised the majority of the total population. What is more, in Europe and America urbanization had more profound social consequences, since those who departed the countryside for the city usually did not return. Such migrants helped to change the city, and in turn the environment in which they lived modified their behavior, attitudes, and actions. In short, they became urbanized, if not urbane. In Russia, on the other hand, the development of cities and life within them was very much under the thumb of officialdom from the middle of the seventeenth century until well into the nineteenth. Peasant rural–urban migration was customarily monitored through permits and passports, and thus a peasant's sojourn in the city was intended to be short-term. The traditionally seasonal nature of residence in the Russian city was by no means restricted to the peasantry. Other members of urban society, and especially the social elite, were similarly peripatetic. Until late in the nineteenth century rural – urban migration was both age and sex selective. The typical migrant was male and between twenty and forty years of age. Figure 1 depicts the migration fields for the major Russian cities in 1897. For St. Petersburg, Moscow, and Odessa especially, migrants frequently journeyed long distances

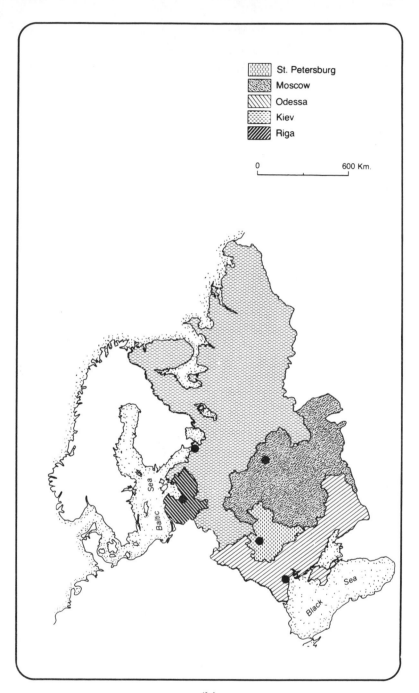

St. Petersburg
Moscow
Odessa
Kiev
Riga

0   600 Km.

Baltic Sea

Black Sea

24

despite the ofttimes short duration of their residence in the city. Clearly the attraction of cities in late imperial Russia was considerable.

At mid-nineteenth century few towns in Russia were very large. Only St. Petersburg, Moscow, and Odessa had more than 100,000 inhabitants. By 1914 about thirty cities had reached that threshold. St. Petersburg and Moscow, with respectively a shade more and a shade less than two million inhabitants, completely dominated the urban system (Figure 2). Three cities, Riga, Kiev, and Odessa, with populations ranging from 500,000 to 700,000 comprised a second level in this system. A network of provincial centers made up the third level in the urban hierarchy. The role of industry varied enormously between cities and regions. Some cities were transformed during the years of rapid industrialization. Others were largely bypassed, remaining dependent upon local commerce and trade, or on government administrative functions, for economic development. Before we examine some of the consequences of rapid industrialization for the two cities of interest here, some of the general features of industrialization in late imperial Russia will be briefly outlined.

Industrialization

By the middle of the nineteenth century there were about ten thousand manufacturing establishments with just over one-half million workers. In most important sectors of industry, however, private enterprise played a decidedly minor role. The state was not only a major market for industrial goods, it was a major producer as well. Government-initiated development policies after the Crimean War (1853–56) culminated in a period of frenetic industrialization around the turn of the century. Although the figures are only approximations, the number of factories and employees increased threefold between 1850 and 1890. Nearly 1.5 million people were now working in over 30,000 factories. By 1913 about 2.6 million workers were employed in the Em-

Figure 1. Migration fields of the major European Russian cities, 1897. *Source: Statisticheskiĭ atlas goroda Moskvy: Territoriia, sostav naseleniia, gramotnost' i zaniatiia* (Moscow, 1911), plate 15.

Figure 2. Largest cities in Russia, 1914

26

pire's manufacturing establishments, that is, nearly twice the figure of 1890. However, the number of factories had increased by only 50 percent in the same period. The concentration of workers in large establishments, already a distinctive feature of Russian industrialization in 1890, was therefore accentuated. In 1910, for instance, more than half of the industrial workforce in Russia was employed in factories with more than 500 workers. In the United States, where economy of scale was the byword, barely one-third of the factory workforce was employed in such large enterprises. Among European countries the share was smaller still. Of course, modernization is not necessarily to be equated with the number of workers in a factory. Compared to both Europe and America, the quality, and cost, of Russian labor was lower. Low wages reflected low productivity. But in some production processes labor could, and did, substitute for more expensive machinery, and this was one reason for such large individual factory workforces. It has also been suggested that because managerial and technical personnel were scarce in late imperial Russia, concentration of production in a single enterprise made more efficient use of the limited available talent. Whatever the reasons, the fact is there were many very large factories. Thousands of workers in a single factory was not uncommon. Indeed, in 1913 a number of factories employed more than 10,000 workers each. The Putilov metalworks in St. Petersburg, for example, was one of the largest. It had more than 13,000 employees. Within the factory was to be found a wide variety of production centers or shops, differentiated by function, skilled labor requirement, and so on. Indeed, the stratification among the factory workforce was considerable. The more urbanized, literate, and skilled the worker, the greater the void between him and the recently arrived peasant. The latter not only stood out by virtue of his calico shirt and high boots; he was frequently motivated by, or more receptive to, different economic and political issues, as Suny and Smith show (Chapters 1 and 3).

The state had long encouraged factories to locate in the countryside. To some extent handicraft activities reinforced the rural orientation of industry since these were mostly found in the villages, especially those of central European Russia where only marginal prospects for earning a livelihood from the land had long ago fostered the development of alternative, nonagrarian

occupations. Thus, a potential labor supply existed in the countryside. But perhaps more important a reason for promoting
rural industry was that many government officials reckoned it
would be potentially less disruptive than urban industry. As it
turned out, this hope was not always realized since strikes and
labor unrest were by no means confined to the city. In encour-
aging industry to locate in the countryside, state policy was in
fact reasonably successful. By 1902, for example, only 41 percent of the 1.9 million factory hands were recorded as living in
cities. In 1914 there were few truly urban-industrial regions in
Russia – St. Petersburg, Moscow, and Riga perhaps being the
most notable exceptions. Together these three areas accounted
for around 18 percent of the Empire's total factory workforce.

As Figure 3 demonstrates, there was considerable regional
variation in the distribution of industrial activity in Russia in the
early 1900s. The area around Moscow was the most heavily in-
dustrialized, yet even here the majority of people still worked
the land. The Baltic ports of St. Petersburg and Riga were major
industrial centers, more spatially concentrated than the Moscow
region, and more modern. Textiles dominated the central industrial district, focused on the city of Moscow, while in the St.
Petersburg and Riga industrial regions metallurgy and engineering accounted for most factory jobs. Metallurgy and food
products industries, notably sugar beet refining, characterized
the industrial structure of the Ukraine. As Figure 3 indicates,
industry was especially dominant in the eastern region of the
Ukraine. Much of the total value of industrial production here
emanated from the heavy metallurgical centers attracted to the
coking coal found in the Donets Basin. In the Baku region the
petroleum industry was particularly important, and in the Urals
mineral resource exploitation was the source of most industrial
employment.

Table 1 reveals that by the early 1900s the Empire's industrial
structure remained dominated by the traditional sectors – textiles and foodstuffs. Still there were some signs of modernization. The metallurgical industries, particularly steel and engineering, had developed quickly and now commanded a sizable
share of the total industrial employment. The expansion of the
metalworking and machinery sector was very much associated
with the program of railroad construction initiated after the di-

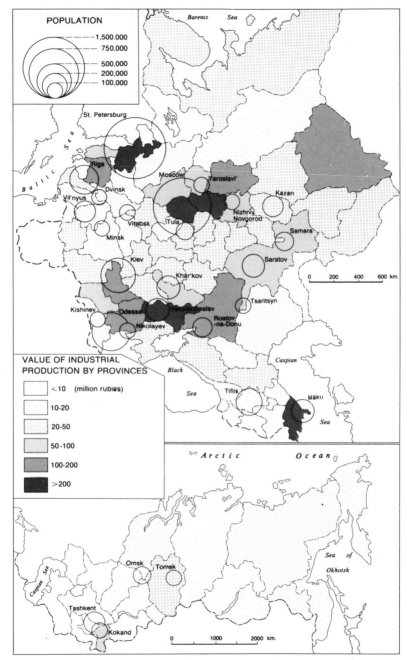

Figure 3. Urban industrialization, 1910

29

Table 1. *Share of industrial employment and production in Russia,*
1897 and 1908

Industrial group	Workers (%)		Gross value of production (%)	
	1897	1908	1897	1908
Textiles	30.6	36.5	33.3	29.8
Food products	12.2	17.1	22.8	33.9
Mining and metallurgy	25.9 }	24.5	13.9 }	16.4
Metalworking and machinery	10.2 }		10.9 }	
Timber processing	4.1	4.1	3.6	3.7
Livestock products	3.1	2.8	4.7	3.5
Ceramics and building materials	6.8	—	2.9	—
Chemical	1.7	2.9	2.1	3.8
Paper	2.2	3.9	1.6	2.8
Other	3.2	8.2	4.2	6.1
Total	100.0	100.0	100.0	100.0

Source: Olga Crisp, "Labour and industrialization in Russia," in *The Cambridge Economic History of Europe; The Industrial Economies, Capital, Labour and Enterprise; The United States, Japan and Russia,* ed. Peter Mathias and M. M. Postan (Cambridge: Cambridge University Press, 1978), vol. 7 pt. 2, p. 354.

sastrous Crimean War. At mid-nineteenth century Russia could boast of barely 1,600 kilometers of railroad. By 1910 there were more than 66,000. The expansion of the rail network drew whole regions into the world of national, and indeed international, markets. The demand for rails and rolling stock helped to shift the traditional emphasis on production of consumer goods, like textiles and clothing, to producer goods, that is, items that are not in themselves end products but are used to manufacture other commodities. Consumer goods from rural handicraft, or *kustar,* industries continued to find a market. Of course, when factory technology was applied to the manufacture of the same commodities, *kustar* production was rarely able to compete in terms of price, and suffered accordingly.

A massive influx of foreign capital, especially from the late 1890s on, made possible the modernization of the industrial structure suggested by the growth of the metalworking, machinery, and chemicals industries shown in Table 1. Foreign investment flowed in largest volume into those industries where growth potential, and profits, were greatest. Mining, electrical engineering, rubber, chemicals, petroleum – all are examples of industries dominated by foreign capital. In many instances, government support through tariff protection or lucrative contracts further boosted profits for foreign investors. Capital investment on the part of Russian entrepreneurs in the early 1900s was still concentrated in the traditional areas of industrial enterprise – textiles, clothing, woodworking, tobacco, and food products.

Only a small share of the Empire's total workforce actually toiled amidst the din and dust of the factory. But in absolute terms the numbers involved were still huge, and given the transient nature of at least a part of the factory labor force, many more people than the 2.6 million operatives counted in manufacturing establishments in 1913 would have had firsthand acquaintance with factory production. Of course, industrialization was much more than just factories and workers. For the recently arrived peasant whose life had been governed by the seasons, the regularity of habit dictated by the factory whistle and clock was an entirely new, and not necessarily welcome, experience. The factory changed the conditions of employment for those who had some work experience in the city; those who had worked in trade, commerce, or domestic service moved from close personal relationships, good or bad, to impersonal, bureaucratic ones, thereby creating a void between owner or manager and employee. Industrialization also required new financial structures and more transport facilities, if not new modes; it destroyed some handicraft activities and spawned others. Put simply, industrialization transformed in both subtle and obvious ways the whole of the national economy. It was both an example and an agent of modernization, and there were a few parts of the Empire that did not experience some of the changes set in motion. But it was in urban Russia that the impact of industrialization was most evident, not least of all in St. Petersburg and Moscow.

St. Petersburg and Moscow

Perched on the edge of the Empire, St. Petersburg, founded by Peter I in 1703, was to be a planned city, one that was to embody

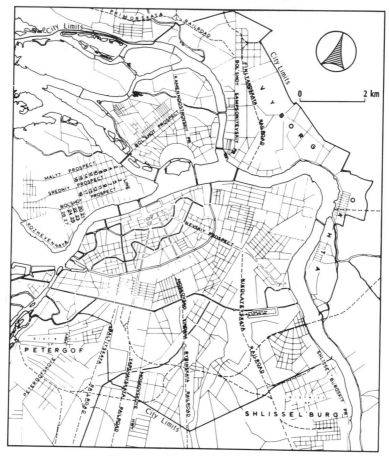

Figure 4. St. Petersburg, 1914

all that was new in architecture and design. And to a considerable degree the central parts of the city did evolve more or less in accordance with prescribed plans. Broad thoroughfares, grand architectural ensembles, restrictions on building heights, setbacks, and materials used in construction, all served to demonstrate the impact of the planning process on the physical fabric of the place (Figure 4). Even though the existence of serfdom made the building of the city possible under the most adverse physical conditions of situation and site, it was scarcely consonant with the prevailing modes of social organization in those

European countries whose technological and military modernity Peter I wished to emulate. St. Petersburg acquired many of the trappings of European town planning, but the fabric of civic society was fashioned according to the precepts of serfdom long after its formal abolition in 1861.

Throughout the later imperial era the legacy of grand design and imperial munificence, the existence of the court, and the ostentation of the upper classes sustained images of grandeur. Yet the reality of daily life for the masses was all too often abject poverty and material squalor. As the capital's population grew tumultuously during the final years of the imperial era, there emerged more clearly than ever before a dual economy. On the one hand, there was ample evidence of modernity in the form of industrialization, commercialism, and all the associated technologies. But in many ways this all lay like a thin veneer over a society whose values remained those of the countryside rather than the city. To be sure, there were peasants who were second generation artisans, factory workers, clerks, and so on, but who remained peasants according to the official classificatory procedures. Many were urbanized. But most peasants were not, and still flocked to St. Petersburg and then back to the village in a rhythm dictated by the seasons.

For many people St. Petersburg embodied Europe in Russia, much as Peter I had intended, but it was not a welcome intrusion. Its peripheral location symbolized the degree to which it was removed from what was truly Russian. Moscow, on the other hand, located as it was in central European Russia, was a city whose history was bound up with the fortunes of the Eastern Slavs, a city that in real and imagined ways was set apart from St. Petersburg (see Figure 2). The rectilinearity of the latter's street pattern contrasted sharply with the seeming hotchpotch inherited by Moscow (Figures 4 and 5). To the extent that the one's architecture was European, the other's was Russian. St. Petersburg served as Russia's administrative heart, Moscow its soul. Indeed, Moscow's skyline adorned with church cupolas, and the constant ringing of bells, together registered graphic first impressions of the city in colorful contrast to those of the capital. Moscow was Russian in other ways as well, including the extent to which Russian as a language was used – in business, in society, and by its inhabitants. Among the social elite of St. Petersburg

Figure 5. Moscow, 1914

Russian was seldom in vogue, and sophistication was not infrequently equated with European manners and language. In the
world of business, knowledge of Russian alone was a handicap.
Foreigners themselves were very much a part of the St. Petersburg scene, and during the decades of rapid industrialization
their influence became all the more pervasive. In Moscow the
role of indigenous enterprise was predominant, something reflected by the industrial structure of the city. As well, the Moscow business elite was more civic minded, more philanthropic,
than its St. Petersburg counterpart. The state and its administrative apparatus naturally influenced urban development in St.
Petersburg to a far greater degree, and thus the city was the
beneficiary of a greater share of state investment, to say nothing

of the impact of the presence of the imperial court. Moscow remained in popular perception and idiom a vast village. Yet Moscow's population was no more peasant in composition than St. Petersburg's.

All told, in the eyes of the ardent Slavophile there was scarcely anything Russian about the capital, and hence little to redeem it. That St. Petersburg and Moscow were both popularly referred to as "capital" was not unrelated to such feelings and perceptions. By the same token, for others who sought the modernization of Russia and its society, St. Petersburg and its European attributes, however superficial, represented a break with the past and thereby held out the prospect for transforming this backward, rural Empire into a modern state. That the Russian city, and notably St. Petersburg and Moscow, should serve as the theater for so much political and social discontent in the last years of the imperial era is no mere coincidence. While one can hardly ascribe to the city a deterministic role in history, the nature of the urban environment bore mute testimony to the need for change.

In the years down to the Great War of 1914–18 conditions in the city, in the workplace, and in the home, were little improved; indeed, they frequently deteriorated further as each year witnessed still larger numbers of people to be absorbed. Higher levels of literacy, rising expectations, and a growing recognition of the inequalities produced by the autocracy's felt need to perpetuate the status quo, all served to underscore the need for change. The many concessions that the revolution of 1905 was instrumental in wringing out of a shaken autocracy simply reinforced the perception among the masses that change was perhaps possible, especially if confrontation occurred on a large enough scale. For the hundreds of thousands who migrated to both "capitals" to escape the poverty of life in the village, the harsh reality of urban existence must surely have sharpened their awareness of inequity. In any event, with the chaos produced by the Great War, the fabric of society began to come apart and culminated in the upheavals of 1917. St. Petersburg and Moscow figure predominantly in this period of Russian history. What follows is a brief outline of the impact of industrialization on these two cities and the nature of the urban environment.

Table 2. *Industrial structure in Moscow, 1913*

Industrial group	Number of establishments	Per-centage	Employ-ment	Per-centage
Metalworking	343	27.3	38,742	20.9
Chemical	80	6.4	6,692	3.6
Food and tobacco products	136	10.8	28,741	15.6
Tanning, tallow, and soap	75	6.0	9,309	5.0
Paper and printing	276	21.9	18,505	10.0
Textile	249	19.8	67,251	36.3
Miscellaneous	98	7.8	15,988	8.6
Totals	1257	100.0	185,228	100.0

Source: D. P. Kandaurov, *Fabrichno-zavodskie predpriiatiia Rossiiskoi imperii (iskliuchaia Finliandiiu)* (Petrograd, 1914).

Industrial structure

In 1913 the factories in St. Petersburg employed close to 195,000 workers; in Moscow there were about 185,000 factory hands. Although broadly the same in terms of the share of factory workers of the total population, there were striking differences in the historical importance of industry as an employer and in the composition of the industrial structure in each of these cities.

As noted earlier, traditional sectors in manufacturing dominated the central industrial district of European Russia, of which Moscow was the focus. Within the city the textile industries still engaged the largest number of workers in 1913 (Table 2). Textiles had always been important in Moscow and at mid-century this sector employed 39,000 of the nearly 46,000 workers in the industrial labor force. Most firms were owned by families, a feature to persist through the years of amalgamation and the rise of the joint-stock company. At mid-century textiles were also the predominant industrial activity in St. Petersburg, but the total industrial labor force was less than 20,000. The metalworking sector employed around 3,900 people, about twice the number in Moscow. This was significant because in both relative and absolute terms the industrial structure of the Empire's capital city

Table 3. *Industrial structure in St. Petersburg, 1913*

Industrial group	Number of establishments	Per-centage	Employ-ment	Per-centage
Metalworking	284	29.7	77,816	40.0
Chemical	89	9.3	16,446	8.5
Food and tobacco products	100	10.5	20,528	10.5
Tanning, tallow, and soap	49	5.1	8,455	4.3
Paper and printing	312	32.6	23,230	11.9
Textile	86	9.0	43,931	22.6
Miscellaneous	36	3.8	4,178	2.2
Totals	956	100.0	194,584	100.0

Source: D. P. Kandaurov, *Fabrichno-zavodskie predpriiatiia Rossiiskoi imperii (iskliuchaia Finliandiiu)* (Petrograd, 1914).

was already more oriented toward what would prove to be the leading growth sector, metalworking.

Table 2 indicates that on the eve of the Great War textile firms continued to employ the largest number of workers in Moscow. Metalworking, especially machine production, however, had increased substantially in the late imperial era. But in St. Petersburg metalworking firms now employed almost twice as many people as textile plants, approximately 78,000 as compared to 44,000 (Table 3). Growth since 1890 had been tumultuous, aided in large part by government contracts for shipbuilding and supplying armaments. Foreign capital was a conspicuous element in the financing of the numerous joint-stock metalworking firms, something that seems not to have occurred with quite the same frequency in Moscow. As a comparison of the share of employment by industry group in the two cities makes plain, Moscow's industry was now the less specialized (Tables 2 and 3).

With about 10,000 more workers, but 300 fewer establishments, St. Petersburg was also different in terms of the scale of individual enterprises. On average each factory in St. Petersburg employed 203 people in 1913. In Moscow the comparable figure was 147. The very large-scale textile plants, now largely under the control of joint-stock companies, were primarily responsible for pushing the capital's average plant size to more than 200 workers. In 1913 each textile plant engaged on average 511 people. In Moscow the still predominantly family-owned factories employed an average of 270 workers. The largest metalworking plant in Moscow had 2,900 people on the payroll; in St. Petersburg pride of place in this sector was held by the Putilov Company, which in 1913 had more than 13,000 workers. As in the case of the capital's textile industry, joint-stock metalworking factories predominated. They accounted for half the labor force and nearly three-quarters of the value of output. Even though the average plant size of 274 workers was substantially below the textile sector, it was more than twice Moscow's figure (113) and was clear evidence that economies of scale played an important role in corporate decision-making. As already noted, the large-scale plant was typical of Russian industry as a whole.

The industrial structure of Moscow is generally assumed to have been less influenced by mechanization than St. Petersburg's, a feature that has been linked to the conservatism characterizing the business practices of the typical Moscow industrial enterprise. To be sure, far more small-scale, family-owned factories were found in Moscow than in St. Petersburg. Indeed, even among the huge joint-stock firms, it was not uncommon for the control of shares to remain in the hands of the founding family. The tendency not to replace labor so readily with machinery gave rise to the characteristic lower level of productivity per worker that provided further contrast between Moscow industry and St. Petersburg industry.

The cupolas of Moscow's many churches had long dominated the city's skyline, as did the spire of the Admiralty and the dome of St. Isaac's Cathedral in St. Petersburg, but by the late imperial era the impact of industrialism was equally palpable. The skyline in both cities was now punctuated by innumerable chimneys belching out one of the more obvious by-products of manufacturing. Notwithstanding the existence of zoning regulations intended to circumscribe spatially the location of industry in St. Petersburg, by the early 1900s there were few parts of the city into which industry had not intruded. But heavy industry was concentrated to the south and northeast and had given rise to grimy factory districts. The same geographical pattern obtained in Moscow, as Figure 6 makes plain. But in both cities factories and their workforces were present everywhere, even though in neither did industry dominate the employment base. We might

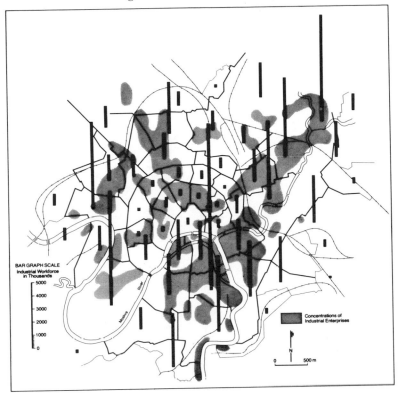

Figure 6. Concentration of industry and workforce, Moscow

turn our attention at this point to some of the consequences of
rapid urban industrialization, bearing in mind, of course, that
although industrialization was the catalyst in rapid urban growth,
the consequences were shouldered by all who lived in these
cities.

Population growth

It is apparent from Figure 7 that the tempo of urban growth
after 1890 was especially rapid in Moscow and St. Petersburg.
Whereas from 1870 to 1890 per annum growth averaged about
15,000 people, thereafter it steadily increased and averaged ap-

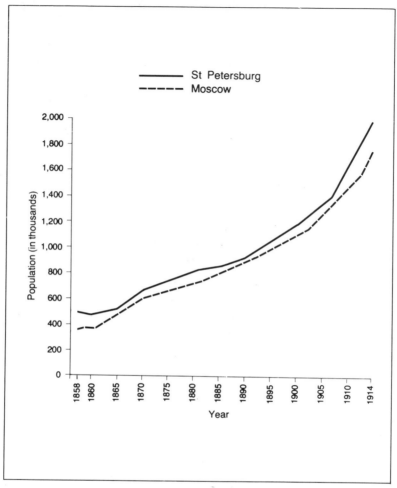

Figure 7. Population growth of Moscow and St. Petersburg, 1858–
1914

proximately 50,000 for each of the six years from 1908 to 1914.
In Moscow, for example, the absolute numbers added each year
translate into percentage growth rates of 2.6 percent per annum
between 1897 and 1902 and just over 4 percent per annum between 1907 and 1912. Averages like these of course mask even
larger absolute and relative increases that characterized particular years. More than 107,000 people were added to St. Peters-

burg's population in 1913 for instance, an increase of more than 5 percent. A surplus of births over deaths helped to swell the numbers, but this was a recent phenomenon and of limited absolute importance.

The relationship between birth and death rates in Moscow and the capital, St. Petersburg, differed little during the latter part of the nineteenth century. Birth and death rates in St. Petersburg in 1870 were 29 and 33 per 1,000 population, respectively. Thereafter, the death rate was slowly reduced so that by the turn of the century it was often in the low 20 per 1,000 range. Inasmuch as the birth rate remained fairly constant, natural increase began to be a regular occurrence by the mid-1880s. This demographic transition was delayed a few years in Moscow. However, in both cities natural increase played a small part in population growth. Between 1870 and 1914 immigration accounted for more than four-fifths of the total increase in population.

As noted earlier, males between twenty and forty years of age comprised the bulk of migrants. Age–sex structures of the urban populations were distorted accordingly, as Figure 8 indicates. Females gradually assumed a more important part in the migration process, especially after the turn of the century, but even so there were still more males than females in each city in 1914. In Moscow, for example, there were only 755 females for every 1,000 males in 1897. By 1912 the number of females had increased to 843 and by 1917 to 982. The change from 1912 to 1917 was, of course, related to the conscription of men during the Great War and the resultant recruitment of women and children to work in the factories in their absence. Within both cities the predominance of males was spatially biased with notable concentrations in those districts with military garrisons and numerous factories. As well, if a particular borough served as a principal destination for migrants owing to job or housing opportunities, its demographic profile was influenced accordingly. For instance, in St. Petersburg the second ward of Spasskaia borough was notable for its multitude of shops, markets, and cheap accommodation, all of which served as a magnet for newly arrived male peasants looking for work. The Khitrov market area of Moscow (in Miasnitskaia borough) was perhaps even more notorious than the Haymarket area of St. Petersburg, but catered to a similar type of male migrant with similar demographic

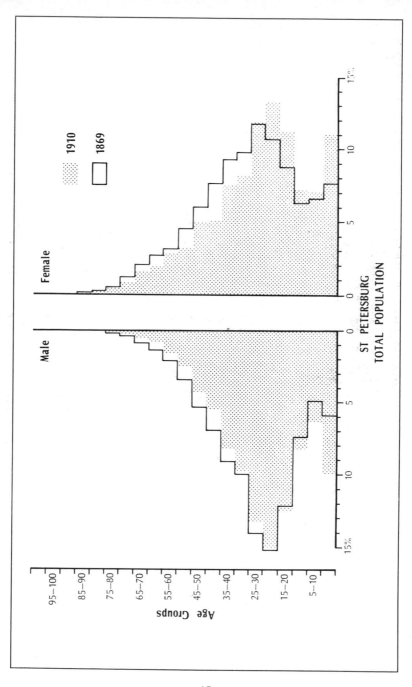

ST PETERSBURG
TOTAL POPULATION

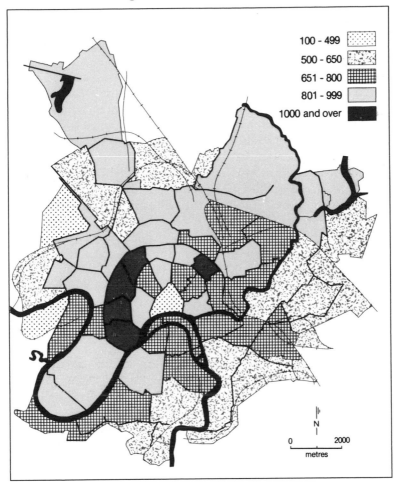

Figure 9. Females per 1,000 males, Moscow, 1902

consequences for the borough as a whole. Here there were only 769 females per 1,000 males in 1902 in the second ward where the market itself was found. Thus, while males dominated the population profile in each city, there were considerable variations in male–female ratio among boroughs, as Figure 9 illustrates for Moscow.

Figure 8. Age–sex profile of St. Petersburg population, 1869 and 1910

Among immigrants, members of the peasant estate *(soslovie)* were numerically dominant. Indeed, by 1914 nearly three-quarters of the inhabitants of Moscow and the capital belonged to this estate, a twofold increase in barely one-half century. While the huge number of peasants the cities had to absorb each year posed one set of problems for civic administration, the high proportion of transients among all inhabitants posed yet others. But just what were the dimensions of transient behavior in Moscow and St. Petersburg? Censuses and city directories help shed some light on this important behavioral trait.

The 1902 census of Moscow indicates that less than 28 percent of the almost 1.1 million inhabitants were native born. Of the 72 percent who had migrated to the city, more than one-fifth, or about 169,000 people, had lived there for one year or less (Figure 10). Almost half of the total migrant population of nearly 791,000 people had been in Moscow for five years of less. Clearly, a substantial proportion of Moscow's population in 1902 had not lived there long enough to develop much of an attachment to the city as a place.

Equivalent data for the capital's migrant population in 1900 and 1910 indicate that the general pattern established for Moscow obtains for St. Petersburg as well. The share of the total population actually born in St. Petersburg was small. In 1900 it comprised about 32 percent of the 1.4 million inhabitants; in 1910 it accounted for about the same proportion of the citizenry, which now numbered 1.9 million. Most migrants were recent arrivals, males were predominant, and peasants completely overshadowed all other estates. Moreover, as the St. Petersburg censuses reveal, a large proportion of this massive inmigration did not put down permanent roots in the city.

The total number of migrants who, in 1900, had lived in St. Petersburg for five or fewer years totaled 414,951. This same group appears in the 1910 enumeration, by that time having been resident in the city for eleven to fifteen years. But in 1910 this group had been reduced from 414,951 to 143,591. Apparently 65 percent of this migrant category had departed the city or died during the 1900–10 period. Given the usual age of migrants, it is probable that most had departed the capital under their own locomotion.

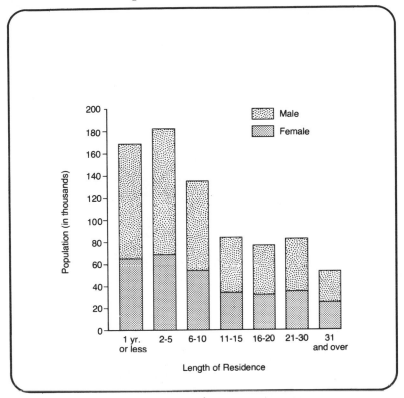

Figure 10. Length of residence in Moscow of all non–Moscow-born inhabitants, 1902. *Source: Perepis' Moskvy 1902 goda* (Moscow, 1904), pt. 1: *Naselenie,* pp. 6–7.

Of course, the suspicion is that migrant peasants account for the greatest number of departures. Since the St. Petersburg census separates peasants from *meshchane*, that rather amorphous estate encompassing elements of the urban middle bourgeoisie, an examination of the general dimensions of transience can be carried a little further. A comparison of the number of peasants who had lived in the city for five or fewer years in 1900 with the eleven to fifteen years residence category in the 1910 census indicates an absolute drop in number from about 325,000 to 115,300 (see Figure 11). Once again, about 65 percent of the group had departed or died. Though the meschane, who comprised 15.5

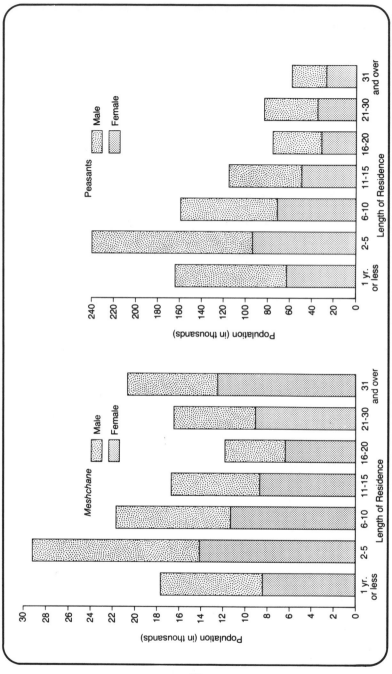

46

percent of the total population in 1910, were ostensibly more urban-oriented, and thus less transient in behavior, more than half their number had migrated to the capital (Figure 11). Using the same procedure as applied to the peasant estate reveals that nearly 60 percent of the group arriving in the 1896–1900 period were no longer resident in the city in 1910. In short, although more of the meshchane than peasants were locally born, the estate apparently was not without its transient element either. The census data obviously intimate that transience was widespread. An examination of some city directory evidence demonstrates that such behavior was by no means restricted to the lower orders.

The use of city directories for the purpose of establishing levels of transience has some major disadvantages. The most obvious defect of the directory as a source is the fact that only a small percentage of the population is listed in the personal section. For Moscow and St. Petersburg on the eve of the Great War the coverage was about one-tenth of the total populations. Moreover, the listings are decidedly unrepresentative of the urban social-class structure. However, by assuming that those who were listed were among the most stable element of the population, then the collective habits of this more likely elite than lower-order segment of the population might well tell us something about both the social-class basis and dimensions of transience.

The data presented in Table 4 are based on a sample of 1,500 males drawn from the 1909 St. Petersburg directory and traced in the 1912 edition. For Moscow a similar sample was drawn from the 1910 directory and traced in the 1913 edition. One of the most striking features of the data presented in Table 4 is the rather large proportion of the sample populations that could not be traced in the later directory. About one-third of the St. Petersburg sample had apparently departed the city or died during the three-year period. It is unlikely that very many died in such a short time-span. It is possible, of course, that some of these seemingly transient individuals were simply omitted from

Figure 11. Length of residence in St. Petersburg of non–St. Petersburg-born meshchane and peasants, 1910. *Source: Petrograd po perepisi 15 Dekabriia 1910 goda* (Petrograd, 1914), pt. 1, pp. 290–3, 302–5.

Table 4. *Residential persistence and mobility,*
St. Petersburg and Moscow

	Same address		Different address		Not listed	
	No.	%	No.	%	No.	%
St. Petersburg 1909–12	553	36.9	448	29.9	499	33.2
Moscow 1910–13	484	32.3	359	23.9	657	43.8

Source: Systematic sample of 1,500 males drawn from *Ves' Peterburg na 1909 g.* (St. Petersburg, 1909) and *Vsia Moskva, Adresnaia i spra-vochnaia kniga na 1910 god* (Moscow, 1910). The sample populations were then traced in the 1912 edition of the St. Petersburg directory and the 1913 Moscow edition.

the ensuing directory. But this probably would not have been a very large number, for each year witnessed a sizable increase in the coverage. Indeed, it would seem that being listed was not just growing in popularity but in importance as well, for Moscow and St. Petersburg were fast approaching the two million population mark, and for such large urban centers directories were now an arguably indispensable feature of urban life. The share of the Moscow sample that could not be traced, almost 44 percent, was even larger than for St. Petersburg. In short, among the ostensibly more stable element of the population, that which was listed in the city directory and tended to be strongly biased toward the top rather than the bottom of the social-class hierarchy, transience was an ingrained habit. Moreover, among those who could be traced, moves from one residence to another within the city were common. For St. Petersburg and Moscow, respectively, about 30 and 24 percent of the sample populations had changed address at least once during these three-year periods. During the early 1900s it is evident that transience of one kind or another played an important part in the urban growth process.

Housing

In the early 1900s, and especially during the years of frenetic industrialization after 1908, a growing proportion of workers were obliged to secure their own housing in the open market. Whereas in the early 1900s a larger proportion of Moscow's industrial workforce still lived in factory-owned housing, workers in both Moscow and St. Petersburg confronted generally similar circumstances. Housing construction lagged behind demand, and rents escalated in consequence. Most contemporary accounts emphasize the resultant carving up of available housing space into smaller and smaller units until renting a corner of a room, or even a bed for part of the day, was the only alternative for those wishing to remain within easy walking distance of their place of work.

In 1913 the average workday in a factory was ten hours. Despite a steady contraction in the length of the legal workday in industry, buoyant economic conditions after 1907 had necessitated overtime work in many plants. Time also must be added for dinner breaks, frequently as long as an hour and a half, and for the journey to and from work, conceivably as long as an hour. In sum, the average factory worker in Moscow and St. Petersburg could well have spent thirteen or fourteen hours each day in work-related activities. Given the generally limited disposable income of the working classes and the high cost and comparative backwardness of prevailing public transport technology, the lack of spatial mobility within the city was a major contributing factor to the generally abysmal levels of overcrowding and congestion.

If conditions were poor for those who were employed in factories, it perhaps should be noted that among the total labor force, factory workers were often comparatively well off. They were also, of course, a minority. Most hired labor in St. Petersburg was engaged in construction, transport, handicraft, trade, and institutional and personal service. Including day laborers, a total of some 500,000 people were involved, roughly two and one-half times the factory workforce. In Moscow the ratio was about the same. Among the nonfactory labor force sixteen-hour working days were quite common. Rates of pay and conditions of employment were often rather worse than in the cities' factories. With dependents, hired labor comprised more than half the total population in Moscow and St. Petersburg.

The rapid population increase during the quarter-century down to the Great War far outstripped the resources of both municipal governments. A crisis of numbers loomed already in the 1870s. The rapid conversion of previously uninhabited cellars and the year-round occupancy of suburban summer houses testified to the pressure on available housing. Jerry-built tenements mushroomed in response to the demand for accommodations. Rents escalated, and overcrowding was pervasive.

Ratios of persons per apartment are the only available measure of the degree of overcrowding. Although admittedly very crude, they do provide some instructive insights into the state of the housing scene. In Moscow in 1882, an average of 9.7 persons resided in each apartment. By 1912 the ratio had dropped to 8.7, indicative of some slight improvement. However, this ratio covers all sectors of the housing market and especially understates the degree of overcrowding among the poor. The masses continued to endure conditions of overcrowding seldom encountered in Europe and America. Only the abysmal state of housing in St. Petersburg could rival that in Moscow.

Whereas it is not possible to qualify population per apartment ratios by taking into consideration the actual floor space involved, comparisons with a few of the major European centers with similarly built environments serve to highlight the pressure on the housing supply in Moscow and St. Petersburg. For example, in Berlin, Vienna, and Paris around 1910, an average of 3.6, 4.2, and 2.7 persons, respectively, lived in each apartment. And during the early 1900s, the housing supply in each of these cities grew more rapidly than did the population. On the basis of this rather crude index, it is evident that on average anywhere from two to three times more people lived in each apartment in Moscow and St. Petersburg than in these European cities. Quantitative measures of congestion obviously tell only part of the story. The actual state of public health and sanitation mattered at least as much. It is in this context that the housing shortage in St. Petersburg and Moscow qualified in every sense as a crisis.

Public health and sanitation

That the state of basic municipal services exacerbated difficulties in adequately housing the masses in Moscow and St. Petersburg stands as a matter of record. Still, there is a need to put some of the available data into a comparative context, both with regard to the differences between the two Russian cities and between them and other major European and American centers.

Although expansion of municipal services like water and sewage took place at an unparalleled pace after 1890, the demand and genuine need for such services always outran the supply. On the eve of the Great War, at least a quarter of the apartments in both cities did without the benefit of running water and toilets. And, of course, disparities existed within the cities. Peripheral regions experiencing rapid population growth frequently had neither municipal water nor sewage services. Suburbs outside city boundaries were under a different jurisdiction, the gentry-dominated *zemstvo*, which rarely provided such services. European and American cities tended to be better off in respect to water and sewage, not only in terms of the level of provision but also in terms of quality. Piped water, for instance, was only of real benefit when free from contagion. In St. Petersburg it was rarely safe to consume untreated municipal water. The revamping of Moscow's water supply system in the late 1890s immeasurably improved the situation there, but from time to time it too constituted a public health hazard. Acute overcrowding and inadequate sanitary measures ensured that the maintenance of satisfactory standards of public health remained one of the most serious problems facing municipal authorities throughout the period from 1890 to 1914. While deaths declined in per capita terms over the long run, regular outbreaks of epidemic disease continued to be a part of life in Moscow and St. Petersburg, their impact being rather coldly insinuated by periodic sharp increases in the number of deaths. As we noted earlier, death rates did occasionally drop to the low 20 per 1,000 range; however, during especially severe epidemics, for instance that of 1907–9, they quickly rebounded to the 28 or 29 per 1,000 level.

During the early 1900s death rates not only fluctuated widely, they did so around a mean appreciably higher than in the capitals of Europe and the major cities in America. Infant mortality alone set Moscow and St. Petersburg apart. In 1909 out of every 100 children born in Moscow, 30 died before reaching one year of age. Only 25 out of 100 did not survive the first year in St. Petersburg, but the situation could scarcely be regarded as satisfactory since infant mortality exceeded twice that registered in many major European and American centers. Infectious disease took an especially heavy toll among the young, but spared no age group and frequently claimed one-third of all deaths. During especially serious epidemics this share could be boosted further still. Consumption, pneumonia, scarlet fever, diptheria, and epidemics of cholera and typhus in particular exacted a heavy price. Both cities acquired legitimate reputations as the most pathological urban environments in Europe. To be sure, cities everywhere had to deal with the task of containing infectious disease. But the death rates in Moscow and St. Petersburg clearly testify to the failure of municipal authorities to meet the challenge adequately.

The inhabitants of Moscow and St. Petersburg lived with the almost continuous threat of being caught up in an outbreak of epidemic disease. Muscovites endured thirty-two outbreaks of smallpox, typhus, and cholera in the short period from 1883 to 1917. The record in St. Petersburg was certainly no better; indeed, even more people succumbed annually to infectious disease of one sort or another than in Moscow. During the epidemic-ridden years of 1907–9, infectious disease claimed more than a third of all deaths in the capital, and in 1908 a staggering 47 percent. In Moscow the populace seemed to fare somewhat better. Although more than 20,000 people contracted typhus between 1907 and 1909, the disease proved fatal to fewer persons than in St. Petersburg. In fact, the situation in Moscow compared favorably with a number of major cities of Europe. Moreover, from the 1890s the state of public health in Moscow had steadily improved, a trend more clearly revealed by the statistics on cholera than by the sparse data on typhus. The cholera epidemic of 1892–3 witnessed more than 3,200 cases. The outbreak of 1909–10, however, produced just over 400 cases. Concerted efforts on the part of municipal authorities to improve sanitary affairs, particularly the water supply, had had obvious returns. Still, as the overall death rate continued to hover in the mid-20 per 1,000 range during the early 1900s, with epidemic diseases accounting for between 15 and 20 percent of all deaths, improvements registered were relative. The same, however, could not be said for St. Petersburg. There the incidence of typhus actually increased from the 1890s to 1914, and so, too, did the rate at which people succumbed.

Moscow's municipal authorities, it seems, could claim more success in improving the general state of public health than their counterparts in the capital, St. Petersburg. Time and again, epidemiologists traced the source of infectious disease in St. Petersburg to the impaired water supply. For some observers the swampy site and inclement weather served to explain the poor state of public health in the early 1900s, but such deterministic rationalizations clearly flew in the face of prevailing scientific opinion. Hypercongestion and an impaired water supply ensured the speedy diffusion of disease. Prevailing levels of literacy did not help either.

Literacy

The hazards to public health presented by the state of the urban environment were well documented, and indeed had been so for many years. In editorials and lead articles the daily press in both cities frequently highlighted the problems of epidemic disease, death, sanitation, overcrowding, and the plight of the poor. Much of the reported raw data derived from the efforts of the Sanitary Inspectorate, an organization whose mandate it was to monitor and improve the public health of the community. But its task was made all the more difficult owing to the high degree of transience among such large numbers of migrants who often brought to the city rather unsophisticated, if not potentially dangerous, countryside customs.

In addition, many rural migrants could not read. According to the census of 1897, for example, only 23 percent of the Empire's subjects were literate. Given the rather crude means used to establish literacy, even this figure is conceivably generous. At any rate, the consequences were many. One was aptly described by George Dobson, the long-serving *Times* of London correspondent in St. Petersburg. Writing about the capital just after the turn of the century, he observed that

St. Petersburg is probably the only city in Europe, or perhaps the world, where danger-signals in the form of placards with glaring red letters are posted up on house-fronts, inside tramcars, and in most places of public resort, warning all and sundry against drinking raw water. Nevertheless, the lowest and most ignorant class of the people, especially those coming from the provinces, have the greatest contempt for cholera and for all the precautions taken against it. . . . The author has seen dirty workmen slake their thirst with water dipped out of their greasy caps from the foulest canals of the city, while cautionary notices (stare) them full in the face only a few yards off.[1]

To be sure, the urban population was more literate than the rural. In St. Petersburg, for example, about 62 percent of the total population were deemed literate in 1900, and 69 percent in 1910. In Moscow the figures were comparable. For the population as a whole, barely 59 percent were literate in 1902. For those five years of age or older, 64 percent in 1902 and 70 percent in 1912 were at least able to read. Notwithstanding the real progress in educating children and in teaching adults to read, bear in mind that the shares still illiterate translated into very substantial numbers, about 500,000 and 600,000, respectively, in Moscow and St. Petersburg on the eve of the Great War. Given the truncated nature of the age–sex profile (Figure 8), the majority of these people were adults and not school-age children or infants. Thus, newspaper editorials and public notices were ineffective measures in conveying to the sizable illiterate adult population the risks of contemporary urban life. Moreover, most illiterate members of urban society lived precisely where municipal services were least well developed, and therefore the standards of public health were the most questionable.

There was an inverse relationship between death rates and rent paid per person for accommodations, a rough measure of social-class standing and the quality of the urban area lived in. In very broad terms the cost of accommodations decreased from city center to the periphery. But it would be a mistake to assume that rates of morbidity varied in simple, fixed, and directly in-

[1] G. Dobson, *St. Petersburg* (London, 1910), 110–11.

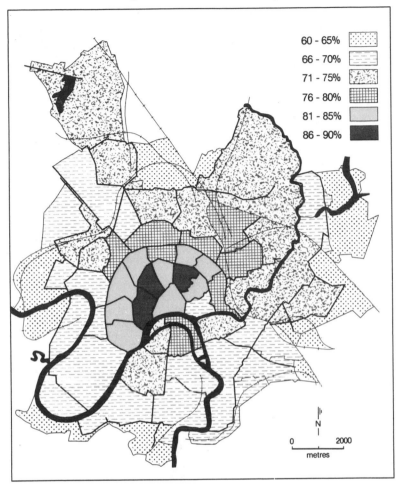

Figure 12. Male literacy in Moscow, 1902

verse proportion from center to periphery. Within the central parts of the city were densely packed pockets of working-class and transient housing, the sanitary condition of which was a contributing factor in producing extremely high levels of disease. However, within the central parts of both Moscow and St. Petersburg there was at least a basic system of municipal services for water supply and sewage. In the peripheral parts of the city, as noted earlier, the development of municipal services was much lower and, combined with factors such as the customarily lower quality of housing and lower level of accessibility, gave rise to lower rents. It was to such accommodations that many recent arrivals to the city gravitated. Not only were they unfamiliar with urban life; being illiterate they were also less able to cope with what was often a pestilential environment. The pattern of illiterate males over five years of age in Moscow in 1902 presented in Figure 12 confirms the general point being made. It is clear that the peripheral wards registered shares of literacy significantly lower than in most of the central city wards. There were some notable exceptions, however; the aforementioned Miasnitskaia borough, in which the Khitrov market was located, was one.

Literacy was often the prerequisite to awakening in the working population a sense of the potential directions for change in society at large, and for forging a sense of solidarity among groups with particular vested interests, be they clerks, printers, or metalworkers. It was also an essential prerequisite for the general enhancement of the quality of urban life. In the early 1900s, however, change of any kind was not readily accommodated by the autocracy and the social, economic, and political structures upon which it rested.

Summary

The conditions of daily life and labor among the masses in St. Petersburg and Moscow were generally difficult and not infrequently dangerous to health and well-being. Urban industrialization came late to Russia and quickly brought to the fore most of the possible defects of the large city, only some of which were touched upon in this chapter. Existing institutions for urban governance and the prevailing attitudes toward city life in many ways were ill-adapted to the changes set in motion. Cities starved for funds, few citizens could participate in local government, and those holding the franchise seemed disinclined to exercise their prerogative. Data assiduously gathered by government authorities pointed very clearly to the dimensions of both demographic change and the impact of numbers on municipal services. But the combination of a highly transient, substantially illiterate pop-

ulation unaccustomed to the hazards of city life and a quite inadequate municipal water and sewage system guaranteed that
the reputation of Moscow and St. Petersburg as strongholds of
disease and death remained intact.

To a considerable extent, the values of society in the late imperial era still bore the impress of the landed aristocracy. Prince
and peasant alike retained real links with the countryside, though
not necessarily for the same reasons. Given that the yoke of serfdom had been shaken off only a few decades before, and given
that it is far simpler to introduce changes legislatively than psy-
chologically, the retention of such traditional values and perceptions is not altogether surprising. But as the ensuing chapters
indicate, change was in the air. Already the upheavals of 1905
had shaken the autocracy to its very roots. World war and the
events of 1917 ultimately put an end to the old order and ush-
ered in the new. In all of this, St. Petersburg – Petrograd after
the outbreak of war – and Moscow figured prominently.

PETROGRAD

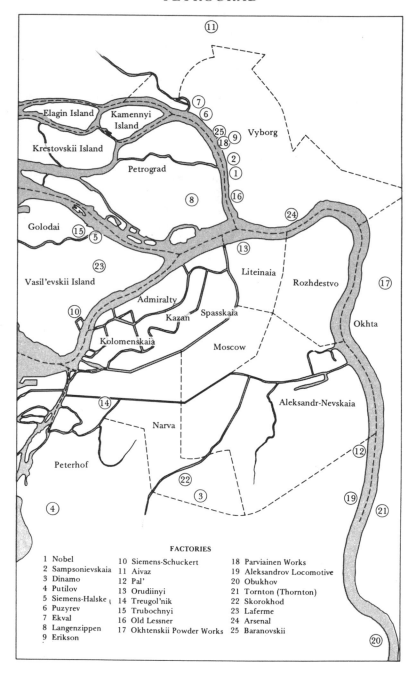

FACTORIES

1 Nobel	10 Siemens-Schuckert	18 Parviainen Works
2 Sampsonievskaia	11 Aivaz	19 Aleksandrov Locomotive
3 Dinamo	12 Pal'	20 Obukhov
4 Putilov	13 Orudiinyi	21 Tornton (Thornton)
5 Siemens-Halske	14 Treugol'nik	22 Skorokhod
6 Puzyrev	15 Trubochnyi	23 Laferme
7 Ekval	16 Old Lessner	24 Arsenal
8 Langenzippen	17 Okhtenskii Powder Works	25 Baranovskii
9 Erikson		

3

Petrograd in 1917: the view from below

Steve A. Smith
University of Essex, England

The city, its industry and workforce

Petrograd was the capital of the Russian Empire and the foremost financial and industrial center in a overwhelmingly agrarian society. In 1917 it had a population of 2.4 million, making it by far the largest city in Russia. The city had been built by Peter the Great as Russia's "window on the West." Its Western architecture and layout symbolized the incorporation of Russia into Western culture and the European state system. Here was the seat of government, the court of Nicholas and Alexandra, the major institutions of learning and the arts, of law, commerce, and industry. In the central districts of the Admiralty, Kazan', and Liteinyi stood the palaces of the most eminent aristocratic families, the apartments of the gentry and wealthy bourgeois, elegant emporia, banks, and company offices. Yet just across the Neva River, to the northeast, were the slums and teeming factories of the Vyborg district; and encircling the city (moving in a clockwise direction) were the predominantly proletarian districts of Okhta, Nevskii, Moscow, Narva-Peterhof, and Vasil'ev-

I wish to acknowledge my debt to the authors of the following works on whose fine scholarship I have drawn freely: Marc Ferro, *The Russian Revolution of February 1917* (London: Routledge and Kegan Paul, 1972); Marc Ferro, *October 1917: A Social History of the Russian Revolution* (London: Routledge and Kegan Paul, 1980); Tsuyoshi Hasegawa, *The February Revolution: Petrograd 1917* (Seattle: University of Washington Press, 1981); David Mandel, *Petrograd Workers and the Fall of the Old Regime* (London: Macmillan, 1983); Alexander Rabinowitch, *The Bolsheviks Come to Power* (New York: W. W. Norton, 1976).

skii, where poverty, overcrowding, and disease were rife. Here there were few open spaces, and no proper roads, pavements, water supply, sewage system, or street lighting. Rubbish was piled up in the streets and open cesspools posed a mortal threat to public health.

With the outbreak of war in 1914, Petrograd became the major center of armaments production in Russia – meeting two-thirds of the nation's defense requirements. The industrial workforce grew by 60 percent to reach 392,800 by 1917 (or 417,000 if one includes factories in the suburbs of the city). Most of this expansion took place in industries producing directly for the war. By 1917 no fewer than 60 percent of the workforce were employed in the metal industries, compared to 11 percent in textiles and 10 percent in chemicals. About half the workforce were newcomers to industry, made up of peasants drawn from their ailing villages by the prospect of lucrative work in industry, and of women responsible for the support of families now that husbands and brothers were at the front. Many of these newcomers had strong ties to the countryside and their experience of urban and factory life was limited. They were a different breed from the skilled men who had worked in industry for many years, whose wages were fairly good and who were reasonably educated and politically aware. No fewer than 68 percent of the city's workforce worked in enterprises of more than a thousand workers – a degree of concentration unparalleled elsewhere in the world. The concentration of experienced, politically aware workers in large units of production was critical in facilitating the mobilization of the working class in 1917.

Under the old order, Russian workers had few of the rights that workers in the West enjoyed – the rights to strike, to form independent trade unions, and to negotiate collectively with employers. During the war the disciplinary regime within industry – especially in those enterprises owned by the government itself – became especially repressive. Although the wages of most workers in Petrograd rose until the winter of 1916–17, their working conditions generally deteriorated. Working hours increased along with the intensity of work, resulting in a huge rise in industrial accidents. Those brave enough to challenge the situation courted transfer to the front, arrest, or dismissal. Workers known to have connections with the revolutionary underground were especially at risk. Yet in spite of the harsh reprisals of the employers and the state, the level of strikes and revolutionary activity rose steadily, as conditions of work deteriorated and as the level of carnage at the front mounted. Even so, in the winter of 1916, notwithstanding the vociferous protests at the dwindling bread supply, rising food prices, and the seemingly interminable war, few would have dared predict that within months the Romanov dynasty would come crashing down.

The February Revolution: dispensation in the factories

The revolution of February 1917 came unexpectedly. It began on February 23 [March 8], International Women's Day, when thousands of angry housewives and women workers, ignoring pleas from labor leaders to stay calm, surged onto the streets. A worker at the Nobel engineering works in the Vyborg district recalled:

We could hear women's voices in the lane overlooked by the windows of our department: "Down with high prices!" "Down with hunger!" "Bread for the workers!" I and several comrades rushed at once to the windows. . . . The gates of No. 1 Bol'shaia Sampsonievskaia mill were flung open. Masses of women workers in a militant frame of mind filled the lane. Those who caught sight of us began to wave their arms, shouting: "Come out!" "Stop work!" Snowballs flew through the windows. We decided to join the demonstration.

The next day 200,000 workers were on strike in Petrograd. By February 25 armies of demonstrators were clashing with troops, and the revolution had commenced. On February 27 the climax came when whole regiments of the Petrograd garrison deserted to the insurgents. The same day, the highly respectable leaders of the Duma refused to obey an order from the tsar to disperse and, with the reluctant support of the army generals, they declared themselves a Provisional Committee ("Government" from March 3). On March 3 Nicholas II finally agreed to abdicate, and Russia was free.

In 1905 the autocracy had withstood the revolutionary movement for nearly twelve months before finally moving to crush it; in February 1917 the autocracy succumbed in fewer than twelve

days. The difference lay in the fact that in 1905 the army had
basically remained loyal to the tsar, whereas in 1917, after three
years of bloody and senseless war, the soldiers threw in their lot
with the insurgents on the streets. Victory became assured once
the liberal conservative opposition agreed to dispense with the
tsar, believing that only thus could the war be won and the revolutionary movement halted.

The downfall of Nicholas "The Bloody" filled the workers and
soldiers of Petrograd with joy and elation. They had no real sense
of this as a "bourgeois" revolution, with all that that implied.
Instead they believed that Russia was embarking on a democratic revolution that would bring enormous benefits to the common people. A general meeting at the Dinamo works declared:

> The people and the army went onto the streets not to replace one gov-
> ernment by another, but to carry out our slogans. These slogans are:
> "Freedom," "Equality," "Land and Liberty" and "An End to the Bloody
> War." For us, the unpropertied classes, the bloody slaughter is unnec-
> essary.

At this stage, a majority of workers, trusting implicitly in the
Soviet as "their" representative, and unwilling to risk dissension
in the revolutionary ranks, supported the policy of the moderate
socialists in giving conditional support to the Provisional Government. They made no attempt, however, to hide their distrust
of the latter. The common attitude was nicely summed up in a
resolution from the Izhora works:

> All measures of the Provisional Government that destroy the remnants
> of the autocracy and strengthen the freedom of the people must be
> fully supported by the democracy. All measures that lead to conciliation
> with the old regime and that are directed against the people must meet
> with decisive protest and counteraction.

From the beginning, therefore, workers were distrustful of the
Provisional Government, which they felt to be bound by a thousand threads to landowning and business interests.

With regard to the burning question of the war, workers in
Petrograd also tended at this stage to go along with the policy of
the Soviet Executive Committee. In contrast to the Bolsheviks,
who after April denounced the war as "imperialist" and called
on workers to urge civil war against their own governments, the
Mensheviks and Socialist Revolutionaries – although divided into

"Defensist" and "Internationalist" wings – tended to put the accent not on opposing the war, but on working for peace. They pressed the new government to work earnestly for a democratic peace between the belligerents, who would renounce all indemnities and annexations of territory. The February Revolution strengthened support among Petrograd workers and soldiers for this policy. Lenin described their attitude as one of "revolutionary defensism" in that they were prepared to continue to fight until such time as peace was achieved, in order to defend revolutionary Russia from Austro–German militarism.

Revolution in the factories

On returning to their workbenches after the February strikes, workers proceeded to dismantle the autocratic structure of management in the factories, just as it had been dismantled in society at large. The creation of a "constitutional" factory was seen to be the prerequisite of an enhancement of the status and dignity of workers within society as a whole. Democratization of factory relations assumed a variety of forms. First, hated foremen and administrators fled or were expelled. At the giant Putilov works, for example, where some 30,000 workers were employed, workers thrust the one-time leader of the factory Black Hundreds, Puzanov, into a wheelbarrow, poured red lead over his head, and trunded him off to a nearby canal, into which they threatened to deposit him in punishment for his past misdemeanors. Second, the factory rule books, with their punitive fines and humiliating searches, were torn up. Third, and most important, factory committees were created to represent the interests of workers to management.

In the large state-run enterprises the new committees temporarily took over the running of the factories, since the old administration had fled. On March 13 committee members from factories belonging to the Artillery Department defined the aim of the new factory order as being "self-management by workers on the broadest possible scale"; and the functions of the committees were specified as the "defense of the interests of labor vis-à-vis the factory administration and control over its activities." To our ears talk of control smacks of workers ousting management and running things by themselves, but in Russian the word *control* has the most modest sense of *supervision* or *inspection*. What these workers from the state plants envisaged was not that the committees should permanently run the enterprises, but that they should have full rights to oversee the activities of the official management and be fully informed of what was going on.

In the private sector the activities of the committees in the spring of 1917 were less far-reaching. There they functioned more or less as trade unions, for trade unions did not become properly established in Petrograd until the early summer. The first act of the committees was unilaterally to introduce an eight-hour working day, something that had eluded them in 1905, and to limit or abolish overtime work. Under enormous pressure, the Soviet and the Petrograd Society of Factory and Works Owners formally agreed to the introduction of an eight-hour day on March 10. The committee then proceeded to press for large wage increases to compensate them for the wartime rise in the cost of living. In the half year prior to the February Revolution, wages had fallen in real terms by about 10 percent as a result of rocketing prices. Now a combination of action by the committees and spontaneous strikes persuaded the employers to agree to increases in monthly earnings of between 30 percent and 50 percent. Having achieved these increases, the committees then settled down to a wide range of activities, which included guarding factory property and maintaining law and order in the working-class districts; checking that workers had been legitimately excused from military enlistment; organizing supplies of food; maintaining labor discipline in the workshops; organizing educational and cultural activities; and campaigning against drunkenness.

Workers and the Provisional Government

The first sign of a growing rift between the masses and the Provisional Government came in April – over the question of the war. Although the government had affirmed its support for the peace policy of the Soviet Executive Committee, on April 18 the Minister of Foreign Affairs, P. N. Miliukov, sent a note to the Allies, which became public on the twentieth, in which he reiterated Russia's determination to fight the war to a victorious conclusion and to stand by the treaties concluded with the Allies, whereby Russia stood to gain Constantinople and the Dardanelles. The publication of this note sparked an explosion of indignation in the factories and barracks. Workers and soldiers poured onto the streets on April 20 and 21, and there were violent clashes with bourgeois counterdemonstrators. The effect of the "April Days" was to deepen popular distrust of the government. Two thousand workers at the Siemens-Halske engineering works demanded the "strengthening of control over the government" by the Soviet Executive Committee, and the "exclusion of the supporters of an annexationist war, in particular, Guchkov [Minister of War under the first Provisional Government] and Miliukov." Other workers' resolutions demanded the renunciation of the secret treaties and the immediate formulation of peace terms.

In an effort to increase its popularity among the masses, the Provisional Government proposed to the Soviet Executive Committee that it join a new coalition government. At first, the Soviet leaders opposed the proposal, since they feared that as ministers they might become compromised in the eyes of the masses. The leader of the Executive Committee, I. G. Tsereteli, however, became convinced of the advantages of a coalition government, and on May 1 the Executive Committee agreed to the proposal by a vote of forty-four to ten with two abstentions. (The opposition came from Bolsheviks, Menshevik Internationalists, and Left Socialist Revolutionaries.) Six socialists thus took up seats in government alongside the ten "capitalist" ministers. It seems that a majority of workers considered that the Soviet Executive Committee had taken the right step in order, as the Admiralty workers put it, "to increase socialist influence over the organs of power." An ominously large minority, however, condemned the coalition as a "ministry of compromise with the bourgeoisie."

At the time of the February Revolution the Bolshevik party had been in considerable disarray. Its most able leaders were abroad or in exile; its membership had dwindled as a result of wartime persecution by the authorities; and the party organization was fragmented, both geographically (there was little centralized coordination of the regional organizations) and politically (factionalism was rife). The February Revolution took the Bolsheviks by surprise, and they divided in their attitude to the Provisional Government. It was only after Lenin returned from Switzerland on April 4 that a meaningful degree of political unity was restored in the party. Lenin's *April Theses* represented an extreme but perspicacious analysis of the political situation in Russia, which broke sharply with the orthodox Social-Democratic conception of a two-stage revolution. Lenin considered that the "old Bolshevik" formula that the "bourgeois revolution is not yet completed" was "obsolete." He argued that a transition to socialism was on the agenda in Russia, since it was the weak link in the international chain of imperialism, and that revolution in Russia would precipitate revolution in the more advanced countries. Thus there must be absolutely no support for the capitalist Provisional Government: power must pass instead into the hands of the proletariat and poor peasantry via a republic of soviets. Meanwhile, Lenin argued, the war remained one of "imperialist banditry," which the Bolsheviks must unbendingly oppose. The Party accepted these new strategic perspectives at its April Conference only after considerable opposition had been overcome; the new views were concretized in the slogans "All Power to the Soviets!" and "Down with the War!"

These perspectives had a tremendous impact, since they accorded with the deepest aspirations of the most radical element within the Petrograd proletariat – the skilled metalworkers of the Vyborg district and, to a lesser extent, of Vasil'evskii Island. The attitudes of these workers found vivid expression in a resolution passed by general assemblies of workers at the Puzyrev and Ekval' factories during the "April Days":

The government cannot and does not want to represent the wishes of the whole toiling people, and so we demand its immediate abolition and the arrest of its members, in order to neutralize their assault on liberty. We recognize that power must belong only to the people itself, i.e., to the Soviet of Workers' and Soldiers' Deputies as the sole institution of authority enjoying the confidence of the people.

Support for the Bolsheviks began to grow from this time, not only in reaction to political events but also to economic developments. By the summer the national economy was staggering under the crushing burdens of war. Production of fuel and raw materials plunged, leading to acute shortages in the centers of industrial production – shortages that the paralysis of the transport system aggravated. The result was that factories began to shut down, and the grim prospect of unemployment faced thousands of workers. Meanwhile the decline in grain production, combined with the chaos on the railways and waterways, led to a growing shortage of bread and basic foodstuffs in the cities. Finally, the dearth of primary items of subsistence, together with an ill-conceived financial policy by the government, fueled inflation to the point where the monetary system eventually collapsed. The Soviet historian, Z. V. Stepanov, reckons that by October 1917 the cost of living in Petrograd was 14.3 times higher than in 1913, and that the real wages of workers had fallen by anything from 10 percent to 60 percent from their January 1917 level. Some workers were already on the verge of destitution.

By the summer of 1917 the trade unions were reestablished, and it was they who led the battle to restore workers' living standards. Throughout 1917 they remained less influential than the factory committees, but they did become important mass organizations. Most were industrial unions, representing the interests of all workers in a given industry regardless of their trade. From the early summer, they began to negotiate with the appropriate section of the Society of Factory and Works Owners to achieve city-wide contracts regulating the wages of all workers in a given branch of industry. Despite acrimonious negotiations with the employers, most unions did succeed in winning such contracts; but although they appeared to grant sizable wage increases, especially to the low-paid, in real terms ravaging inflation devoured these increases almost before the ink had dried on the contract.

The deteriorating material condition of workers, especially of the low-paid, produced a radicalization in the political attitudes of the less skilled, less well off peasant workers and women workers. This was especially apparent at the Putilov works, where low-paid workers vented their anger and frustration on trade union and factory committee leaders whom they felt to be too dilatory in promoting their interest. I. N. Sokolov, a Bolshevik at Putilov, reported: "The mass of workers in the factory . . . are in a state of turmoil because of the low rates of pay, so that even we, the members of the works committee, have been seized by the collar, dragged into the shops and told 'Give us money!'"

In general, however, economic distress tended to make workers receptive to Bolshevik attacks on the capitalist system, the imperialist war, and the bourgeois – landlord government. On June 20 S. M. Gessen informed the city committee of the Bolshevik party that:

the Putilov works has come over decisively to our side. The militant mood of the factory has deep economic roots. The question of wage increases is an acute one. From the very beginning of the revolution the workers' demands for wage increases were not satisfied. Gvozdev [a Menshevik and deputy to the Minister of Labor] came to the factory and promised to satisfy their demands, but he did not keep his promises. On the demonstration of June 18 [organized by the Soviet Executive Committee, supposedly to rally support], the Putilov workers bore placards saying "They have deceived us!"

The rising tide of militancy among individual workers came to a head at the beginning of July.

The armed demonstrations of July 3–4, known as the July Days occurred against a background of worsening economic difficulties, the dismal failure of the June offensive launched by Kerensky in order to impress the Allies, the attempt of the government to remove to the front regiments stationed in Petrograd, and the breakdown of the coalition government after the resignation of four Kadet ministers. The demonstrations were organized from the grass roots, but after initial wavering, the Bolshevik party agreed to assume leadership of them. The aims of the thousands of workers and soldiers who took to the streets were apparently straightforward – to force the resignation of the "ten capitalist ministers" and compel the Soviet Executive Committee (or more correctly, since the First All-Russian Congress of Soviets, the Central Executive Committee) to form a government. Events quickly took a nasty turn. Clashes broke out between demonstrators, counterdemonstrators, and government troops, in which as many as 400 were killed or wounded. On the night of July 4–5 the government – now under the leadership of Kerensky – in a determined effort to prove to the propertied classes its fitness to govern, arrested leading Bolsheviks, such as Trotsky and Lunacharskii, forced Lenin and Zinoviev to go into hiding, ransacked the Bolshevik party headquarters, closed *Pravda*, and rounded up arms in the possession of workers. Shortly thereafter the Kerensky government reintroduced the death penalty at the front and announced its intention of restoring discipline in the army. The July Days thus ended not in a soviet government, but in the Provisional Government taking a sharp turn to the right.

The July Days, even though dramatically illustrating the outright hostility of the majority of workers and soldiers to the government, highlighted their ambivalence toward the moderate socialists who controlled the national network of soviets. The demonstrators hoped to force the Central Executive Committee to take power; but the committee was determined not to do so and denounced the demonstrators as "counter-revolutionaries." This created confusion among the latter, evidenced in the speech of one of four workers allowed to address the Central Executive Committee on behalf of fifty-four factories:

It is strange to read the appeal of the Central Executive Committee: workers and soldiers are called counter-revolutionaries. Our demand – the general demand of the workers – is all power to Soviets of Workers' and Soldiers' Deputies. . . . We demand the retirement of the ten capitalist ministers. We trust the Soviet, but not those whom the Soviet trusts. Our comrades, the socialist ministers, entered into an agreement with the capitalists, but these capitalists are our mortal enemies. . . . The land must pass immediately to the peasants! Control of production must be instituted immediately! We demand a struggle against the starvation that is threatening us!

"We trust the Soviet but not those whom the Soviets trust." In his fine study, David Mandel calls this the "paradox" of the July Days. The demonstrators had to believe that the Executive Committee could be persuaded to take power, since they could see no other alternative, yet the Central Executive Committee was prepared to lose popular support rather than assume power.

It is likely that a majority of workers still did not abandon hope in the Central Executive Committee, for the bloodshed and fraternal strife of the July Days strengthened a desire for unity against the openly mobilizing counterrevolution. For a short time, the Bolsheviks lost support as workers reacted against their divisive policies. Nevertheless, once everyone had time to take stock, workers – especially those in the metal industry – concluded that the members of the Soviet Central Executive Committee were "traitors" who had joined the ranks of the class enemy.

Workers' control and Bolshevism

Meanwhile, throughout the summer a movement for workers' control of production was built up. Workers' control is often depicted as an anarchist-inspired attempt by workers to seize the factories. In fact it originated as an eminently practical effort to stem the tide of economic disorder and to keep the factories running. The agents of workers' control, the factory committees, at first confined themselves to trying to procure fuel and raw materials and to keeping a general eye on management. During the summer, however, as the economic crisis deepened, the committees became convinced that the employers were deliberately exacerbating the crisis in order to quell workers' militancy and to make them "see sense." In a bid to stamp out "capitalist sabotage," the committees instituted more far-reaching forms of control. They took to intervening actively in management affairs, by examining order books and financial accounts, and insisted that all decisions made by the administration be ratified by the committees. In so doing, the committees sought to keep the factories open and to stave off mass unemployment. The Soviet historian, M. L. Itkin, estimates that by October 289,000 workers in Petrograd – or 74 percent of the industrial workforce – worked in enterprises under some form of workers' control. This should be kept in perspective, however, for Itkin calculates that workers' control operated in only ninety-six enterprises, which must mean that nearly 90 percent of Petrograd enterprises – mainly small and medium workplaces – were untouched by it.

The big employers could not tolerate such incursions on their "right" to manage as they saw fit. Consequently, they pressured Minister of Labor M. I. Skobelev to take steps to curb the factory committees' efforts at workers' control. Skobelev responded by issuing two circulars that forbade the committees to interfere in the hiring and firing of workers or to meet during working hours – a move that provoked howls of protest from the workers. The Langenzippen workers resolved:

Skobelev's circular has a purely political character and is counter-revolutionary. It prevents the labor movement from following an organized course and supports the organized march of the conter-revolution, which aims to sabotage industry and reduce the country to famine. We are forced to conclude that the Ministry for the "protection of labor" has been converted into the Ministry for the "protection of capitalist interests."

As a Menshevik, Skobelev believed that workers' control could only aggravate disorder in the economy, since it involved uncoordinated actions by atomized groups of workers. The moderate socialist argued that only planned centralized regulation of the economy by the state could begin to undo the damage wrought by the war. The Bolsheviks, too, believed that only action at the central level could restore the battered productive forces, but they argued that it was folly to trust this to a capitalist government, since any restoration of economic order would inevitably be at the expense of working people. They thus supported workers' control, essentially as a means of mitigating economic disorder until such time as a workers' government took power. Their support for workers' control was a major cause of the party's growing popularity. Indeed the factory committees were the first of the popular organizations to come out in favor of Bolshevik policies. As early as the end of May at the First Conference of Petrograd Factory Committees, a resolution drafted by Lenin "on measures to combat disruption in the economy" won 297 votes to 21, with 44 abstentions. The opposition of the Menshevik and Socialist Revolutionary parties to workers' control, in turn, lost them a lot of grass-roots support.

As class conflict polarized ever more sharply, the Kerensky government was left stranded without any social support. Compared to the upheavals convulsing society, politics was increasingly reduced to a kind of shadow play. Hated by the radicalized masses, Kerensky's new coalition sought support from the Right, only to discover that the Right too was radicalizing. Army officers, industrialists, and middle-class liberals had now come to despise Kerensky for being weak, irresolute, and "soft" on the Left. After the failure of the June offensive they had begun to coordinate the search for a strong man who would crush "anarchy" in society, revitalize the army, and restore order to the economy. In August they found their "man on a white horse" in General Lavr Kornilov, recently appointed Supreme Commander-in-Chief by Kerensky. Kornilov made no secret of his desire for a military dictatorship that would crush the soviets, and plans were laid. The putsch, launched on August 28, failed almost as soon as it began, owing to poor organization, divisions within the counterrevolutionary ranks, and heroic resistance from railway and telegraph workers. In Petrograd the district soviets and factory committees helped to organize bands of armed workers to patrol the city or dig trenches and erect fortifications on the outskirts. Although Kornilov's forces never got within striking distance of the capital, the specter of counterrevolution frightened ordinary working people, who blamed Kerensky for allowing things to come to such a pass. Many were convinced that the extreme situation required an extreme solution.

After the Kornilov rebellion, support for the Bolsheviks grew in leaps and bounds. On August 31 the Petrograd Soviet passed a Bolshevik resolution for the first time, by 279 votes to 115 (with 51 abstentions). This resolution called for a government of representatives of the revolutionary proletariat and peasantry, for immediate peace negotiations, for confiscation of the large estates, and the introduction of workers' control in industry. On September 5 the Socialist Revolutionary–Menshevik presidium of the Soviet resigned, and Bolsheviks were elected to a majority of places in the new presidium with Trotsky as chairman. A majority of workers in the factories now supported the Bolshevik program. The Kerensky government – desperately trying to stitch together a new coalition – was deemed in the words of the Admiralty workers to be a "government of bourgeois–landlord dictatorship and civil war, which is conducting a policy of betrayal of the revolution and deception of the people." The moderate socialists of the Central Executive Committee, for their part, were unequivocally denounced for the "ruinous policy of compromise with the propertied classes, who seek to strangle the toiling masses with the bony hand of hunger." The Bolsheviks had dropped the slogan "All Power to the Soviets" after the July Days, since there was no chance of the soviets assuming power under moderate socialist leadership, calling instead for a "revolutionary government of the proletariat and poor peasantry." Some factories followed this change in tactics, and class hostility to the bourgeoisie and to capitalism became far more explicit. On August 10, for example, the Erikson workers demanded "the organization of a genuinely revolutionary power resting on the workers, soldiers, and poor peasants, i.e., a power which will be a dictatorship directed against the counter-revolutionary bourgeoisie." Not all factories followed suit: Many continued to call for a government based on the soviets, or for a "homogeneous socialist government," or for a "homogeneous government of representatives of revolutionary democracy."

A new theme emerged within workers' discourse in September, namely, the need for workers to arm themselves in order to forestall a repetition of the Kornilov adventure. Alongside demands for the freeing of those Bolsheviks still in prison since the July Days, for the disbandment of the Kornilovite General Staff, for the abolition of the death penalty, and for the dispersal of the State Duma and State Council, there figured the demand "to give arms to the workers so that we can organize a Red Guard." The Red Guards were armed detachments based on the factories, which consisted mainly of young men loyal to the Bolsheviks. The Red Guards described themselves as an "organization of the armed forces of the proletariat for struggle with the counter-revolution and defense of the conquests of the proletariat." But it became evident as September dragged into October, and Kerensky continued to cling to the vestiges of power, that the units training each evening in the factory yards were getting restive.

As support for the Bolshevik program grew, so workers flocked to join the party. In April the Petrograd organization had about 16,000 members; by October membership had risen to 43,000, of whom two-thirds were workers. Most of these recruits were young men (there were relatively few women) who were joining a political party for the first time. Some, however, joined from other parties. A Menshevik woman from the Siemens-Schuckert works asked to join the party, saying, "The Menshevik party leaders have forgotten their program and are not fulfilling the interests of the proletariat and poor peasantry. They have restored the death penalty and have locked up the best popular leaders in 'democratic jails'." A Socialist Revolutionary from the Aivaz works wrote to the newspaper *Rabochii (The Worker)*, stating: "Because of profound misunderstanding I joined the SR party which has now passed to the side of the bourgeoisie and lent a hand to our exploiters. So that I shall not be nailed to this mast of shame, I am quitting the ranks of the chauvinists. As a conscious proletarian, I am joining the Bolshevik comrades who alone are the genuine defenders of the oppressed people."

It is easy in retrospect to assume that from now on a Bolshevik victory was inevitable, but Lenin certainly did not believe this. His profound grasp of the social dynamics underpinning the system of "dual power" had allowed the party to turn to its advantage the successive political crises and to win an ever wider circle of popular support, but Lenin was convinced that power would not fall into the lap of the Bolsheviks. It would have to be seized. From the end of September, therefore, from his hiding ground Lenin relentlessly harried the Central Committee to prepare for an armed uprising.

The overthrow of the Kerensky government proved to be a relatively painless affair. At 10 A.M. on October 25 the Military Revolutionary Committee issued the following triumphant message:

The Provisional Government is overthrown. State power has passed into the hands of the organ of the Petrograd Soviet of Workers' and Soldiers' Deputies – the Military Revolutionary Committee, which stands at the head of the Petrograd proletariat and garrison.

The cause for which the people fought – an immediate proposal of a democratic peace, abolition of landlords' property rights in land, workers' control over production, the creation of a Soviet government – this cause is assured.

Long Live the Revolution of workers, soldiers and peasants!

The major factories of Petrograd and the main organizations of labor welcomed the new government. It is true that a minority of workers opposed what they saw as a violent and illegal seizure of power that threatened to engulf Russia in civil war. These consisted mainly of printers, about half the railway workforce, most white-collar workers (e.g., bank employees and draftsmen), and the odd factory such as the Pal' textile mill located in the mainly bourgeois Alexandro-Nevskii district of Petrograd. There is little doubt, however, that the majority of workers were pleased to hear that Kerensky had fled the city. They felt that at last a genuinely revolutionary government had come to power, representative of workers and peasants and based on the soviets. The immediate tasks of this government were clear: to bring an end to the war, to give land to the peasants, and to restore order in the economy. But regarding its longer-term tasks there was

less agreement. Some resolutions passed by workers perceived
the new government as merely a caretaker administration until
the Constituent Assembly should meet. At the other extreme,
some perceived the Bolshevik government as a proletarian dictatorship that would rapidly reorder society on socialist lines.
The majority of resolutions in between were much vaguer: Some
talked of socialism, some of revolutionary democracy. The majority – at least initially – favored a coalition government com-
prising all the parties in the Soviet, since, in spite of massive
disillusionment with the Mensheviks and Socialist Revolutionaries, they continued to be seen as legitimate democratic parties.
At the beginning of November, however, no one foresaw that
the country would soon be ruled by a one-party dictatorship and
be poised on the threshold of civil war.

Conclusion

Until recently, much Western historiography has presented the
October insurrection as a military coup carried out by a tightly
knit minority party, led by a man with an almost Nietzschean
will to power. There is an important grain of truth in this view.
For the overthrow of Kerensky was indeed a well-organized coup
carried out by the Bolshevik party at the behest of Lenin: To
that extent, the October Revolution was quite unlike the February Revolution, when the masses themselves had directly precip-
itated the final crisis of the *ancien régime*. But to depict the October insurrection as a coup pure and simple is to fail to plumb
its essence. The dominant characterization of the events of October 24–25 deserves closer scrutiny.

In October 1917 the Bolsheviks were still a minority party. In
the national elections to the Constituent Assembly in November,
they gained only a quarter of the vote, as against 38 percent for
the Socialist Revolutionaries and 13 percent for the Kadets. Popular sentiment, however, was still shifting in the Bolsheviks' favor. In June only 105 Bolsheviks had been elected to the First
All-Russian Congress of Soviets, as opposed to 283 Socialist Revolutionaries, 248 Mensheviks, and 73 nonparty delegates. At
the Second All-Russian Congress of Soviets on October 25 – before the walkout of the moderate socialists – there were 390 Bol-

sheviks, 160 Socialist Revolutionaries, 72 Mensheviks, 14 Internationalists, 6 United Social Democrats, and 7 Ukrainian Social Democrats. By October support for the Bolsheviks was overwhelming in the large industrial centers, especially Petrograd, in the garrisons of the rear and at the front. Workers and soldiers were the most solid supporters of the party. Most groups of workers – with the exception of certain "labor aristocrats" and white-collar workers – had swung behind the party, beginning with the skilled metalworkers but quickly followed by unskilled peasant workers and women. It was in the vast rural areas that Bolshevik forces remained weak. But even there, the peasants who voted for the SRs in the Constituent Assembly elections voted for the policies of the left-wing of that party (which had already split from the "conciliationist" wing), and on the crucial questions of the land and the war, Left SR policies were not dissimilar to those of the Bolsheviks.

Until recently in the West, the workers, soldiers, and peasants were seen to have played an essentially destructive, anarchistic, and elemental role in the revolution. They were the "dark masses," able to tear down but not to build. Typical of this view is the comment by Theodore von Laue that "Russian politics from May 1917 to the spring of 1921 . . . must be viewed primitively in terms of Hobbesian social mechanics, in terms of crude violence among masses uprooted by war and revolution." The recent work of historians such as Diane Koenker, David Mandel, Ronald Suny, William Rosenberg, and Alexander Rabinowitch dissents from that view. The changing attitudes and activities of Petrograd workers, at least, are perfectly comprehensible in essentially rational terms, without resort to some Hobbesian model. The workers had very concrete needs and expectations that the Provisional Government failed to meet. They turned to the Bolsheviks because their policies seemed to represent the only viable political alternative.

Of course, rational self-interest does not exhaust the meaning of the revolution: In fact, it provides a rather jejune explanation of working-class conduct in 1917. Workers were motivated by more than mere calculations of means and ends. Their rationality was deeply imbued with morality and even utopianism. Revolutionary consciousness had emotional and moral, as well as rational, bases. Hope, a sense of justice, hatred, fear, and indignation all played a part in moving workers into action. Yet, in the final analysis, the radicalization of workers in 1917 can be explained quite simply: It arose from the fact that their hopes that the Provisional Government would uphold the interests of the common people, the status of workers in the workplace and in society, achieve a speedy peace settlement, and give land to the peasants, were bitterly disappointed. Instead the government appeared to uphold the interests of the privileged and the system of exploitation and militarism on which their power rested. As the employers and landowners were perceived deliberately to prolong the war, to perpetrate sabotage in industry, and artificially to create the food shortages, so working-class hostility to the propertied classes grew and support for the Bolsheviks increased.

Related to the view of the "dark masses" is the notion that the Bolsheviks won their following by "manipulating" the base instincts of the masses by a fearsome combination of demagogy and lies. To be sure, Bolshevik agitation and organization played a crucial role in radicalizing the masses. But the Bolsheviks themselves did not create popular discontent or revolutionary feeling. This grew out of the masses' own experience of complex economic and social upheavals and political events. The contribution of the Bolsheviks was rather to shape workers understanding of the social dynamics of the revolution and to foster an awareness of how the urgent problems of daily life related to the broader social and political order. The Bolsheviks won support because their analysis and proposed solutions seemed to make sense. A worker from the Orudiinyi works, formerly a bastion of defensism where Bolsheviks were not even allowed to speak, stated in September that "the Bolsheviks have always said: 'It is not we who will persuade you, but life itself.' And now the Bolsheviks have triumphed because life has proved their tactics right."

In respect of the same issue, it is clear that, rather than the Bolshevik party, the working class itself was the major factor in Petrograd politics in 1917. Workers created a gamut of organizations and a huge variety of revolutionary practices that to some degree, constituted the embryo of a new social order. Not only was a national network of soviets set up, first by workers and soldiers and later by peasants, but also factory committees (probably the most important of the proletarian organizations), trade unions, workers' militias, Red Guards, consumer cooperatives, and educational and cultural organizations. Measured against this powerful grid of interlocking organizations, the Bolshevik party apparatus was puny. The Bolsheviks were not, therefore, in any real position prior to October to manipulate or control these popular organizations. Instead the Bolsheviks won support from the organizations by taking up their concerns as the party's own, and gradually rose to positions of leadership within the organizations, largely by democratic means. By successfully relating to the popular movements, the Bolsheviks had, in a sense, already "come to power" even before the overthrow of the Provisional Government.)

Finally, the notion of the Bolshevik party as the "manipulator" of the masses has another source in a stereotyped image of the party itself. This view projects the party in 1917 as being an exact replica of the model party outlined by Lenin in 1902 in *What Is To Be Done?* In this pamphlet Lenin argued for a vanguard party of professional revolutionaries, highly disciplined and centralized, and conspiratorial in its methods. In 1917, for better or worse, the reality of the Bolshevik party was very different. In the first place, it was a *mass* party, with perhaps as many as 300,000 members by October, working openly. Secondly, it was a loosely structured organization, in which the Central Committee had astonishingly little control over provincial and city organizations. Thirdly, the much-vaunted discipline of the party was a fiction. On every major question of the day there were sharp disagreements and factions that did not stop short of frontal challenges to the leadership of Lenin himself (most dramatically, the opposition of Kamenev and Zinoviev to the October seizure of power). The party in 1917 was thus characterized by vigorous debate, a measure of internal democracy, and considerable flexibility with regard to its relations to the masses. Relative to its rivals (which had suffered fatal splits and a massive hemorrhage of members), it is true that the Bolshevik party was more unified and centralized, but it was a far cry from the "organizational weapon" beloved of some political sociologists.

In making a final assessment of the October seizure of power one is forced to conclude that the events of October 24–25 were far more than a military coup. They were the political resolution of a long-drawn-out social crisis, the origins of which go back at least as far as 1905. The war released the accumulated tensions within Russian society, and the February Revolution once more opened up a divide between the popular masses and propertied society. This divide ran so deep through society that the possibilities for bridging it, even in March 1917, were very limited. The Provisional Government, aided by the Soviet Executive Committee, for several months attempted to do so, but it failed to tackle with the necessary speed and nerve the issues that were of pressing concern to the masses. It thus lost any potential social base that it might have had. Instead, it devoted itself to one end – the preservation of the alliance with society – and failed even at that. When in October the Bolsheviks overthrew the government of Kerensky, it appeared to the suffering masses to be less a lethal deathblow to the body politic than an act of euthanasia.

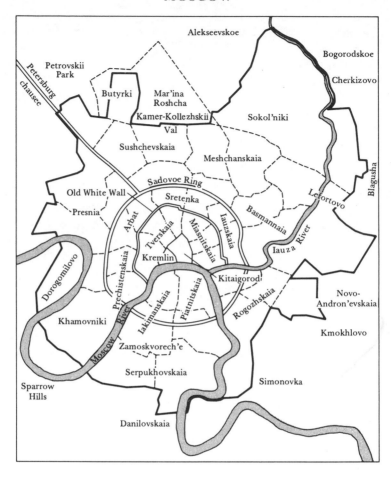

4

Moscow in 1917: the view from below

Diane P. Koenker

University of Illinois, Urbana-Champaign

A powerful aspect of the prevailing view of the revolution – of the white and red contrast between good democratic liberals and evil Bolsheviks – is that it makes the past very simple. This simplicity, in turn, makes the past easier to understand and to express as moral lessons for our own time. The reality of 1917 is much more complex. The revolution of 1917 – any revolution for that matter – should be thought of as a kaleidoscope. Patterns fall into place and then fall apart, and then become reassembled in different patterns. In order to stress this kaleidoscopic aspect of the revolution and to emphasize the many-layered reality of 1917, I shall draw upon my own work on Moscow's working class during the revolution.

When I set out to do a study of Moscow workers in 1917, I had three goals in mind. The first was to study the revolution as it happened away from Petrograd. Petrograd was a unique place: It was the center of political power, the home of the aristocratic elite, the most advanced industrial center in the country, and it was relatively near the eastern front of the world war. All these factors would surely affect the process of revolution in ways that might not be repeated elsewhere. So I turned to Moscow, not just for the sake of learning *what* happened in a different place, but also to understand *why* Moscow's experience was different, if indeed it was. In so doing, I hoped to add a new dimension to the history of 1917.

A second goal, equally if not more important to me, was to examine the revolutionary process of 1917 from the perspective of the workers, in whose name after all the Bolshevik party claimed power. I wanted as much as possible to determine the workers' own attitudes, goals, and behavior, rather than the behavior and goals ascribed to them by their representatives. It is all very well to know that Lenin claimed that the workers in mid-1917 were to the left of the party, but I wanted to know what that meant, if true, and how accurate in general were the leaders' assessments of the mood below. Since the received views of 1917 are based on these assessments, I felt they required corroboration based on workers' sources themselves. If the assessments of people in high places about the workers turned out to be incorrect or incomplete, as I suspected, then my study of the workers could add a further dimension to our understanding of 1917.

Seeing the revolution from below was related to a third goal, which was to demonstrate in the context of 1917 the value of the methods of social history, of exploring the history of society. The field of history has come a long way from G. M. Trevelyan's view of social history as "history with the politics left out." What I wanted to show was that the politics could not be understood without first knowing what were the aspirations and realities of life of the many and varied elements that made up society. My example was and is Moscow, but this approach to politics and history is valid for any other historical period, and essential, I believe, for understanding and dealing with the contemporary world.

Revolution in the other capital

Let me consider the first of these three goals, the revolution away from Petrograd. What in fact was so different about Moscow? One cannot really say it was Russia's Chicago, its second city, because before Peter the Great, Moscow had been the capital, the center of Muscovy. It was therefore felt to be quintessentially Russian, whereas Petrograd was a foreign Western City. By 1917 Moscow was a native Russian city whose economic base was mixed and reflected the diversity of central Russia.[1] Textile production

---

[1] On the peculiarities of Moscow, see also Alfred J. Rieber, *Merchants and Entre-preneurs in Imperial Russia* (Chapel Hill: University of North Carolina Press,

was important, but it was balanced by more technologically advanced industry requiring skilled workers, and by a more traditional artisan economy as well. It is significant that half of Moscow's workers were not factory workers at all – they were artisans,
transport workers, workers in the service sector, such as domestic servants, waiters, cooks, barbers, yardkeepers, and the like.
So Moscow was less "proletarian" than Petrograd, if we define a
proletarian as a worker employed in a large modern industrial
plant. Of course, the other crucial feature of Moscow is that it
was not the capital. The most important politicians, diplomats,
generals, and leaders of political parties tended to base their activities in Petrograd where decisions were made and power was
to be had.

These factors colored the experience of Moscow's revolution.
In general, political leaders in Moscow were more moderate, more
inclined to compromise, than were their Petrograd counterparts. This holds for rightist parties as well as left-wing Bolsheviks. Perhaps political moderation was due to the fact that the
really committed ideologues preferred to be in Petrograd, and
those who remained in Moscow were more practically minded.
But Moscow's moderation was also due to the social makeup of
the city. There was more diversity and less polarity within society
and within the working class, and the diverse groups exercised
a kind of countervailing power over one another, making com-
promises both possible and desirable. The history of Moscow's
revolution reflected these local factors. On the other hand, Moscow was part of the larger political entity, and what happened
in Petrograd was certainly not irrelevant to Moscow, Saratov, or
wherever the tsar had ruled up to February 1917.

Because Petrograd was in the driver's seat, Moscow has usually received short shrift in general histories of 1917. Trotsky
has a few dismissive things to say about Moscow; John Reed took
the train down to Moscow during the October street fighting
because just then it was more exciting there. But is the ignorance

1982); Laura Engelstein, *Moscow, 1905: Working Class Organization and Political Conflict* (Stanford: Stanford University Press, 1982); Robert Eugene Johnson, *Peasant and Proletarian: The Working Class of Moscow in the Late Nineteenth Century* (New Brunswick: Rutgers University Press, 1979); Joseph Bradley, *Muzhik and Muscovite: Urbanization in Late Imperial Russia* (Berkeley: University of California Press, 1985).

of Moscow due to the assumption that Moscow and the provinces were of no importance to the fate of the revolution, or is it
because Moscow, Kazan', Baku, and elsewhere merely repeated
the process patented by the northern capital?

When we learn that the same kinds of revolutionary pressures
existed independently in these towns, that the tsarist government was just as alienated from society, that the Provisional Government was just as inept in local administration as it was in setting national policy, that during 1917 itself the working classes
became increasingly alienated from the middle classes, it be-
comes clear that the revolution was no isolated phenomenon restricted to the weird and un-Russian city of Petrograd.

Let me illustrate with a few examples from Moscow's revolution. The February Revolution in Petrograd evolved over a period of several days of increasing popular disorders, soldiers'
mutinies, and government crises. Panicky officials withheld information from the rest of Russia, but when the news of Petrograd's disorders reached Moscow late on February 27, the old
regime fell virtually overnight. The next day crowds of workers
and well-to-do converged on the city center, attacked and dis-
armed police stations, liberated political prisoners, and began to
form new temporary governing bodies, including a soviet of
workers' deputies. All of this happened within forty-eight hours
of the receipt of the news from Petrograd. Moscow was clearly
ready for revolution, and there were few in the city willing to
defend the old regime. As has been recently pointed out, it was
the news from Moscow that finally convinced Nicholas II that it
was hopeless to try to resist the revolution.[2] Once he heard Moscow had joined the revolt, he agreed to sign his abdication decree.

Afterward, political life in Moscow tended to be less acrimonious than in Petrograd, and the major crises that rocked the capital and created new seeds of discontent were muted in the second city. When moderate socialists agreed to enter a coalition
government in May, Moscow Mensheviks disapproved of their
party's decision, but had no power to influence Petrograd. When

[2] Tsuyoshi Hasegawa, *The February Revolution: Petrograd 1917* (Seattle: University
of Washington Press, 1981), 490.

radical Bolsheviks launched an armed uprising in July in Petrograd, their Moscow counterparts very reluctantly demonstrated in support. Their demonstration was a miserable little affair, carried out only because of loyalty to party discipline. Finally in October, despite important political and economic developments that had brought the Bolsheviks a majority of votes in a citywide election, neither the Right nor the Left was sure how to respond to the seizure of power in Petrograd. There was "Alphonse and Gaston" quality to Moscow's October Days. The Left felt itself to be the natural heir to power, but did not want to fight for it. The Right was just as reluctant to fight to defend its fragile position. Unfortunately, instead of a peaceful stalemate, the mutual indecision led to protracted street fighting engaged in by small numbers on each side. False rumors that reached Petrograd, claiming Moscow's cultural monuments such as the Kremlin had been destroyed by artillery bombardment, together with the news of bloodshed, gave rise to the erroneous impression that Moscow in October was the scene of bitter class conflict.

In reality, political life in Moscow in 1917 was generally more congenial than in Petrograd, but the Provisional Government misinterpreted congeniality for outright support. When in August the government convened in Moscow a huge state conference designed to prop up the faltering regime, government leaders like Kerensky were quite amazed that Moscow's workers had declared a general strike in protest. Restaurant workers would not serve the assembled dignitaries; cabbies would not even drive them from the train station to the Bol'shoi Theater, where the conference was held.

To understand how the situation in Moscow evolved from a sense of revolutionary unity in February to a partisan Bolshevik majority in October requires an examination of the process of polarization that occurred in Russian society. Because even though Moscow was protected by distance from the political squabbles of the capital, indigenous processes of class polarization helped to doom an amicable solution to the revolutionary crisis of power. These processes can be seen very clearly by turning to an examination of the role of the workers.

Social diversity of the working class

The most widespread historical assumption about workers has been that they are simply masses, usually dark masses. In effect, workers are assumed to be undifferentiated, protoplasmic, and sheeplike in their inability to think or act independently of guiding intellectuals. There are two variants of this "mass" label. Those who tend to be sympathetic to the goals of the revolution characterize the workers as "heroic" masses, as "men of marble"; they possess innate creativity, their revolutionary zeal in 1917 grows and expands like a crescendo in a romantic symphony, culminating in a big cymbal crash in October. This is the Soviet view.

On the other hand, those who are less sympathetic to the goals and realities of the 1917 Revolution characterize these same masses as "dark," peasants in workers' blouses, workers who carry with them the peasant tradition of ignorance, violence, and drunkenness. Many well-meaning Mensheviks in 1917 believed this of the working masses, and convinced themselves therefore that Russia was ready only for a bourgeois revolution.

Why should we be concerned whether these assumptions are correct or not? For one thing, we know that society in the twentieth century, even in Russia, was too complex for such simple-minded visions of some ten million people to be true. And more importantly, the fundamental question of the legitimacy of the 1917 Revolution – and, one could argue, the present Soviet state – depends upon a correct assessment of the social forces at work in 1917. So for this kind of assessment, seeing the workers merely as "masses" just will not do.

In fact, when I began to study the workers of Moscow in detail, what struck me most was the diversity of the working class there and the potential for antagonisms and conflicts *within* the class. There were internal conflicts or a potential for conflict along many lines. One division has been relatively widely acknowledged – that between "urban proletarians" and "peasant migrants." In the Menshevik view of things, the urban worker was the model labor aristocrat, a second- or third-generation worker, educated, skilled, socialist, but reformist. The peasants, on the other hand, felt hostility at having been plucked from their familiar villages, and displayed their resentment at their new status by striking out at all symbols of authority. Surely these crude peasants should not be trusted with a revolution.

In fact, many of the assumptions about rural and urban workers have turned out to be unfounded. The newly arrived peasants did not hate the city – it offered them new opportunities, money, and a chance to get away from old granddad down in the village. By the same token, urbanized workers were not necessarily well integrated and reformist – some of them were in danger of losing their jobs because of technological innovations and because industrialists feared their revolutionary potential. If an evaluation of this difference proves important in explaining the revolutionary process, surely other kinds of divisions are also important to examine.

There were potential conflicts between generations, in part because of difference in experience, in part because of processes involved with maturation. A forty-five-year-old metal turner might be less hotheaded in 1917 than his nineteen-year-old son for several reasons: The older worker did not have the energy he used to, he had a family to worry about, and he also remembered too well the tsarist political repression that sent many of his coworkers, if not himself, to jail or exile. The nineteen-year-old son, on the other hand, had few memories of repression; he also had more energy and more economic freedom to take chances, be it on the barricades, in the Red Guards, or as a Bolshevik agitator.

There were conflicts as well between the sexes. Women workers were generally much more passive than men politically. Not only did women work long hours, but they bore the brunt of standing in line for scarce food and keeping a household together while men served in the army. There was also, however, a sense of competition between men and women workers that professional socialists tried hard to eradicate. Women earned less than men, and therefore employers often preferred to hire them rather than have to put up with expensive and sometimes disrespectful males. The presence of women in the labor force thus drove down the wage for all. When we read that striking workers demanded equal pay for men and women, therefore, this could mean several things: The strikers were idealists and thought women deserved equal pay for equal work, or else the strikers hoped that by raising the cost to an employer of hiring women, these workers would no longer be a bargain, and their jobs would return to men.

By the same token, there existed potential conflicts according to skill level – skilled workers feared their replacement by less skilled workers using sophisticated machines. Unskilled workers may well have resented the privileges and prestige of skilled workers. Similarly, there were divisions between those who worked in manufacturing enterprises and those who provided services, between blue-collar workers and white-collar, but poorly paid, clerks, such as postal and telegraph workers.

All these diversities make it difficult to speak of "the workers" or the "toiling masses" in Russia, both before, during, and after 1917. Certain types stand out, however, in terms of their revolutionary activism. Those workers who were most active in political activity – in trade unions, soviet work, factory committees, in strikes – tended in Moscow to be young, male skilled workers, including those from trades that had been considered artisanal or craft-oriented. Peasant migrants tended to defer to such workers as their natural representatives, although these other workers were not absolutely passive and did rise to defend their own interests. Further, the record for Moscow shows that most workers, of whatever type – even women – were drawn into the arena of revolutionary politics in some way or another. The months between February and October represented an intense and dynamic school of political education.

But I would caution against seeing even the urbanized, politically conscious group of workers as leading a great march toward socialist October. These same workers struggled with divisive aspects of the labor movement in 1917 as well as with "class enemies." Different workers' institutions bickered among themselves for leadership roles: Trade unions and factory committees each fought for the right to represent workers on the shop floor, and local soviets competed with local factory committee organizations. The year 1917, in Moscow and elsewhere, saw a host of competing and active grass-roots organizations, of which the Bolshevik party was only one.

Even within the same stratum of the workforce, within individual workers, there appear in 1917 conflicting goals, conflicting values. Take the case of skilled metalworkers. They were at

the forefront of the movement to denounce the war, passed antiwar resolutions by the score, demonstrated against the war, and
supported antiwar positions taken by the Bolsheviks. But they
also earned their livelihood by producing weapons paid for by
the state. When their private employers threatened to close down
production because state subsidies had stopped, the workers
themselves went directly to the relevant ministry to demand a
restoration of the subsidies so their jobs could continue.

All this is to say that in their diversity, Moscow workers were
also human. They were neither men of marble nor ignorant
country brutes. They meant well, they wanted their rights, they
were idealistic. They wanted in all their different ways to shape
their own destiny, but they had different ideas about what that
destiny should look like. The most amazing thing about all these
diverse and various workers was that by October of 1917 they
pretty much all wanted the same thing – soviet power. But the
different segments of the labor force arrived at this conclusion
for different reasons, via different roads.

The issue of soviet power

Soviet power meant that the old institutions – dumas, Provisional Government, and their bureaucratic representatives –
would *not* have power. Some workers believed in soviet power in
principle: They had supported soviet power from the very beginning of the February Revolution, but such workers were in a
distinct minority. Others believed in soviet power for practical
reasons, because the alternative Provisional Government had
failed to solve any of the problems workers felt most strongly
about – the war, the food supply crisis, the collapse of industry,
and the land question.

By keeping a record of all resolutions passed by workers and
published in the Moscow press in 1917, I have been able to trace
the development of support for the slogan, "All Power to the
Soviets!" By summarizing this development, I hope also to con-
vey an idea of the process by which I constructed the history of
1917 in Moscow.

The earliest workers to call for soviet power were the skilled
and already politicized machine-building workers. Throughout

the first half of 1917, when the mood in Moscow was relatively good-humored, these workers continued to support the ideal of soviet power, but almost always in conjunction with some other demand. For example, many resolutions in May and June claimed that only a government of soviets could solve the prevailing economic crisis. Not only were most supporters of soviet power metalworkers, but those passing such resolutions were largely concentrated in a single but major industrial district south of the Moscow River (Zamoskvorech'e).

After the soviets refused to take power during the July Days, enthusiasm for soviet power resolutions declined, but did not disappear, and when the right-wing general Kornilov attempted to seize power in Petrograd in late August, the working-class response was again that only a government of soviets could solve Russia's political and economic crisis. The number of soviet power resolutions peaked in October; at least 50,000 workers passed resolutions in support of power to the soviets. More importantly, textile workers, who had been politically inactive earlier in the year, accounted for one-quarter of the supporters of soviet power. The process of revolutionary mobilization can be seen most clearly when it emerges that most of these textile workers' resolutions came from Zamoskvorech'e, the same radical district that had produced soviet power resolutions from metalworkers earlier in the year. In the northeast Lefortovo district, where many textile workers lived but without many radical metalworkers, no resolutions favoring soviet power were passed. It is possible to conclude that the machine workers helped to catalyze, by their radicalism and their proximity, the more passive textile workers into activism.[3]

A final point that emerges from the soviet power resolutions is that workers did not just vote for them because it was the Bolshevik party line. The same factories that passed soviet power resolutions in, say, July, also elected Menshevik deputies to the Moscow Soviet. The middle months of the revolution, this kind

---

[3] On the relationships among workers of various skill levels, in addition to S. A. Smith, *Red Petrograd* (Cambridge: Cambridge University Press, 1983), see also David Mandel, *The Petrograd Workers and the Fall of the Old Regime: From the February Revolution to the July Days, 1917* (London: Macmillan, 1983), and *Petrograd Workers and the Soviet Seizure of Power (July 1917–June 1918)* (London: Macmillan, 1984).

of analysis reveals, were crucial to the Bolsheviks' building of respect and support. Their policies gained support before their party did. In September and October, finally, workers began to reelect their deputies, giving the Bolsheviks a majority in the city soviet and, it can be assumed, in the mood of the working class at large.

If the call for soviet power by October was a radical solution, Moscow's workers had indeed become radicalized, but the process was incremental, and took place in response to *specific* economic and political factors. Textile workers, for example, did not become radicalized so much because they were dazzled by Bolshevik pie-in-the-sky promises, as some historians would like to think,[4] but because of specific incidents. For example, when a factory manager would announce the shutdown of a plant because there was no fuel left to fire the boilers, a workers' delegation would then investigate all the firm's warehouses and discover ample reserves. The Bolsheviks, almost alone of all the socialist parties, claimed the bourgeoisie could not be trusted, and here was proof. When incidents like these were reported in the press, or discussed in the neighborhood tavern, the process of radicalization by experience spread.

The growth of class consciousness

Underlying this process was a growth as well in class consciousness. By this I mean that the idea of "class," in the strict Marxist sense, became by October the most important organizing principle for the way workers looked at the world. Marxist class analysis had been part of Russian working-class culture since the great spurt of industrialization in the 1890s: It was attractive to non-revolutionary intellectuals as well as to aspiring worker-intellectuals in the late nineteenth century. The rhetoric of class and of class struggle was thus a part of the discourse of working-class life.

The important thing is that in 1917, class analysis worked. Many

[4] See, for example, William H. Chamberlin, *The Russian Revolution*, 2 vols. (New York: Grosset and Dunlap, 1965), 1:275; John L. H. Keep, *The Russian Revolution: A Study in Mass Mobilization* (New York: W. W. Norton, 1976), 95.

of the conflicts of the year could be seen in terms of class struggle; class enemies behaved like enemies, from the capitalist ministers who sent working-class boys to fight the Germans, to the
industrialists who celebrated their name days with sugar cakes
while the workers had to settle for a daily ration of eight ounces
of black bread. The principle of class struggle thus gave structure to the other factors plaguing workers in 1917: The utter
collapse of market capitalism, the vacuum of power, and the inability to end the war could all be interpreted in terms of contradictory class interests.

It is possible to examine the development of class consciousness in Moscow in 1917 by looking at several separate indicators
of working-class attitudes. By filing in a computer information
about factories, resolutions passed in those factories, political
contributions, and strikes, I have been able to keep track of what
kinds of workers engaged in these activities, when they did it,
and what they said.

Resolutions, such as those on soviet power, are not an ideal
measure of political attitudes, since workers usually voted yes or
no for a resolution presented by an outside speaker. But since
there was no Gallup Poll in 1917, these resolutions, if used cau-
tiously, describe significant trends, because they do indicate in a
general way what concerned workers at various points during
the revolution.

In the early months of 1917, there were many resolutions of
cautious support for the Provisional Government. There were
more resolutions demanding that Russia's war goals be clarified
than there were in outright opposition to the war. Such resolutions reflected and helped to foster the spirit of compromise that
characterized Moscow's revolution. But beginning in May, resolutions denouncing the Provisional Government replaced those
supporting it, and the economy supplanted the war as the most
talked-about issue. Inflation began to spiral uncontrollably about
this time, and the number of strikes increased as well. Here in
May was the first indication of how serious the economy and the
question of the management of the economy would become for
political stability.

By August, resolutions began to focus on outright opposition
to the Provisional Government: Workers spoke out against the
Moscow state conference and against the growing indications of

counterrevolution, given substance late in that month with the
Kornilov mutiny. The mutiny, in turn, provoked the greatest
outpouring of protest on any single issue all year.

The tenor of resolutions had changed over time. Early resolutions emphasized working-class interests, but in a context of
mutual give-and-take. By autumn, the resolutions suggest that
workers had diminishing confidence in the government and the
classes that supported it, and they emphasized instead soviet power
and working-class solidarity.

The same picture can be drawn, with somewhat less detail, by
looking at political contributions made by workers. In many factories workers regularly allocated a percentage of their wages to
causes usually decided on by a vote at a general factory meeting.
Lists of these contributions were published in the socialist press.
I have calculated that at least two-thirds of the Moscow working
class participated in this form of political activity, so the nature
of recipients of the contributions provides another excellent in-
dicator of popular mood. The bulk of contributions were directed toward working-class institutions – the soviet, strike funds,
and socialist parties. Early in the year there was a huge outpouring of money in the form of a "Red Gift" to soldiers. This could
be construed as a national rather than a class goal, and I think it
is fair to argue that by making this gift, workers were seeking to
forge an alliance with classes other than themselves, especially
the peasantry. The Red Gift was patriotic, but on the other hand,
it was also red. However, after June the share of contributions
to purely class causes increased dramatically. Even though the
Red Gift may have indicated a populist sentiment rather than a
purely patriotic one, few contributions were made to any military cause after the disastrous Kerensky offensive of June. But
it is also important to note that purely partisan causes – Bolshevik, Menshevik, anarchist, and Socialist Revolutionary – received far less public monetary support than causes representing all workers together, such as the soviet, strike funds, and
especially a general election fund that was to be shared equally
by all three socialist parties. This constitutes strong evidence of
the class orientation of Moscow workers, in the sense that the
whole class was more important than any of its parts.

Finally, the same process of increasing consciousness of class
can be seen in the strike movement. Strikes in Moscow peaked

in the period from May to July and declined thereafter, but more important than the number of workers on strike were the issues of contention. Most strikes concerned wages: Nine out of ten strikes demanded at least in part higher wagers. But toward the autumn of 1917, strikes over workers' control and organization became more frequent and more protracted, and paralleled a shift in political attitudes (by industrialists as well as by workers, by the way): Wage strikes could be seen as part of a normal process of negotiation between capital and labor. Conflicts over job control and trade-union recognition represented a more fundamental conflict about power – about who would have the right to determine work conditions. The decline of strikes in the autumn suggests that certain groups of workers had begun to perceive that this kind of control, this kind of power, could best be won, could only be won in the political arena, not on the factory floor. It is particularly significant that strikes in Russia as a whole by skilled workers, whose sense of politics was often more sophisticated than semiskilled or unskilled workers, almost disappeared by October, whereas strikes by semiskilled textile workers actually peaked in October.[5] Both the strikes of the textile workers and the reluctance of skilled workers to strike represented in different ways the importance of class. Skilled workers had already learned that no compromise could be reached with the entrepreneurial class; semiskilled workers were learning in the process of their strikes and from the experience of others that only concerted, organized, widespread mobilization along class lines could prevent a defeat of their revolutionary hopes. Thus the scale of strikes by autumn was much greater than six months earlier, and the rhetoric of strikers more couched in language about the "labor army" and the unity of the working class. The strike experience, both to participants and observers, thus reflected the depth of polarization along class lines, and the growing identification of class struggle with political revolution.

Thus, through the concrete experiences of 1917, as mediated by the prior influence of Marxist thought, the principle of class struggle helped to reconcile the diversities and antagonisms within

[5] This problem is explored in Diane Koenker and William G. Rosenberg, "Skilled Workers and the Strike Movement in Revolutionary Russia," *Journal of Social History* 19(1985–6):605–30.

the working class. Therefore, it is highly significant that the Bolshevik party *alone* preached the most consistent version of class struggle of any of the socialist parties; as Smith and Suny have noted earlier, the Bolsheviks alone refused to participate in a coalition government together with the bourgeoisie, on grounds that later appeared to be correct: The bourgeoisie, they said, would never honestly cooperate with *its* class enemies, the workers.

It is important to recognize the validity of the view that October represented very real social aspirations. The October Revolution was genuine social revolution as the Bolsheviks maintained and not a coup d'état. I part company with Bolsheviks at this point, however, because I do not believe that class consciousness was a one-way, irreversible process. The class consciousness of October, by the same logic under which it had developed, represented that particular historical moment. When the "class-pure" Bolsheviks, once in power, failed to provide political responsiveness and economic security to the working class, as Rosenberg shows in Chapter 5, nonclass ties, such as regional, ethnic, and occupational and factory bonds, asserted more appeal than class solidarity. Therefore, the consolidation of the Moscow workers around their class representative, the Bolshevik party, was bound to weaken, as it surely did by the end of 1920. Perhaps this is why the Bolshevik leadership felt impelled to continue the rhetoric of class struggle so stridently right up to the second world war: Under Stalin, Mensheviks, Socialist Revolutionaries, Trotskyites, and Bukharinites, were not just enemies of the revolution, they were *class* enemies.

Conclusions

Let me now review the distinctive aspects of Moscow's workers and its 1917 revolution, and then try to suggest what meaning they have for current interpretations of 1917. The first thing to bear in mind is that Moscow was less polarized than Petrograd; there was a spirit of moderation and cooperation that seems to have been missing in Petrograd. Second, and this I think influenced Moscow's moderation, Moscow's workers were not uniformly factory proletarians, peasant migrants, or small shop craftsmen. The Moscow labor force was diverse, and it reflected various levels and kinds of experience. Given this diversity, certain skilled and radical metalworkers – evacuees from Petrograd, in fact – realized that they had to temper their rhetoric in order not to antagonize their less strident fellow workers. Nonetheless, and this is my third point, by October a diverse working class had pretty much rallied around a radical solution to the problems of the revolution. They wanted the soviet, the democratic representative of their class only, to take power and to solve the enormous problems the "all-class" government had been unable or unwilling to solve.

What does this mean for the way we understand the revolution that brought the Bolsheviks to power? First, both the February and October revolutions were popular ones. That February was popular is well known. It is perhaps less well known how much grass-roots support for socialism there was, even at this early stage. But many historians, and even more policymakers who rely on these historians' conclusions, refuse to believe that October was anything more than a coup d'état forced upon a war-weary, revolution-weary people. Studies of the urban revolution, and others on the countryside and provinces, demonstrate the inadequacy of this interpretation.

A revised view of the Moscow revolution also offers some explanations for the popularity of the soviet revolution in October. Moderate socialists helped defeat themselves by not appreciating the huge sentiment in favor of socialism, by distrusting the ability of the workers and peasants to know what was best for them. And, of course, they defeated themselves by drastically underestimating the costs that continuing the war had for a peaceful and moderate outcome of the February Revolution.

For their part, the Bolsheviks demonstrated a far better grasp of the realities of the social revolution in 1917. The Bolsheviks succeeded in winning over the urban working classes by being on the right side of the class issue; they preached class struggle and told the workers they could govern themselves, whereas the Mensheviks kept saying workers did not yet know how to run a country. The Bolsheviks refused to cooperate with other classes in visible but symbolic places such as the Provisional Government; they did participate in lower-level institutions, such as food supply organizations and local councils, perhaps thereby demonstrating their fitness to govern.

The Bolsheviks succeeded, moreover, because they were not terribly doctrinaire. Lenin was important in 1917, but he was not the whole party, and the flexibility of lower-level party activists helped the Bolsheviks to respond better than other parties to the changing terrain of the revolution.[6] The Bolsheviks succeeded because they cared about organization. They were not such die-hard determinists that they felt they could wait until the revolution came to them. And, finally, they succeeded because their strongest supporters – the urban workers – were concentrated where political power was. Once central power passed into the hands of these people, opponents of social revolution in the countryside and on Russia's periphery found it difficult to mobilize the coercive force necessary to stop the revolution.

In terms of what happened in 1917, the Bolshevik party came to power legitimately. If we evaluate the current regime on the basis of how it *came* to power, then we must concede that the Soviet regime represented, and in its symbolism continues to represent, very real and important social aspirations.

However, growing interest by scholars in the period that followed October, the period of the civil war, has suggested that the stamp of the current Soviet regime was not made in October 1917, that the features of one-party rule, of terror, and Stalinist compulsion that influence our perceptions of the Soviet Union today, were not necessarily inherent in the process by which the Bolsheviks *came* to power. Rather, we must look to the critical period after October, at what the Bolsheviks did to *hold* power, in order to assess accurately the sources of the Soviet political system and the nature of its legitimacy.

And just as looking at the goals of social groups and classes helps us to understand 1917, this approach from below will surely prove fruitful in understanding the critical years that followed.

---

[6] This feature of the Bolshevik party has been demonstrated in Alexander Rabinowitch, *The Bolsheviks Come to Power* (New York: W. W. Norton, 1976).

5

Russian labor and Bolshevik power: social dimensions of protest in Petrograd after October

William G. Rosenberg
University of Michigan

The relationship between Russian labor and Bolshevik power in the months immediately following October remains a central and contentious issue of early Soviet history. Bolshevik political legitimacy turns in large measure on the degree to which the party was able in this period to retain the support of workers whose activism in 1917 had brought the Bolsheviks to power; and the nature and extent of workers' opposition to the new regime in these early months is fundamental to our understanding of its dictatorial structure. These issues, central to the work of E. H. Carr, Leonard Schapiro, and others, have recently reemerged in the literature, both implicitly and explicitly. Whereas new books by S. A. Smith, David Mandel, and Diane Koenker on 1917 have examined carefully the social circumstances of Petrograd and Moscow workers, Schapiro's own last volume, *The Russian Revolutions of 1917*, takes sharp issue with historians whose work centers on "social trends, economic theories, or sociological analysis." Roy Medvedev and Vladimir Brovkin have demonstrated how elections to local soviets in the spring of 1918 brought extensive gains for Mensheviks and Socialist Revolutionaries, including popular majorities in all provincial capitals where elections took place;[1] and an important new collection of materials

---

This essay first appeared in *Slavic Review* 44(1985):213–38, and is here slightly revised. Readers are referred to the original version for full documentation.
[1] Vladimir Brovkin, "The Mensheviks' Political Comeback: The Elections to the Provincial City Soviets in Spring 1918," *Russian Review* 42(1983):1–50, esp. 37–8; Roy Medvedev, *The October Revolution* (New York: W. W. Norton, 1979), esp. chap. 12, "The Masses Turn Away From the Bolsheviks."

edited by M. S. Bernshtam for Alexander Solzhenitsyn's series on modern Russian history reasserts an old Right Menshevik view, put most forcefully perhaps by Grigorii Aronson, who maintained that the Bolsheviks had been in power scarcely two months before

all sympathy for them had disappeared, and the benevolent neutrality of the weeks preceding [October] gave way to a committed opposition. . . . After [Brest Litovsk], the convocation of the Constituent Assembly again became a popular watchword. The need for a democratic state power qualified to speak in the name of the entire country was felt more and more. And in the workers' quarters, sympathies for the Mensheviks and SRs revived, after having abated. Thanks to the actions of these groups in the soviets and bolshevized trade unions, and the ideological influence they exercised, the opposition gained the upper hand.[2]

Suppressing the opposition, and "regaining the upper hand" thus became, for Aronson and others, the first requirement of early Bolshevik politics and the cornerstone of "communist autocracy."

The importance of these issues to our understanding of early Soviet history has prompted me to raise them again here, and to examine in particular the validity of conceptualizing labor opposition to the Bolsheviks between October 1917 and July 1918 in essentially political terms. I hope to do this by focusing on several longer-term patterns that I think proved of great importance in these months; by looking closely at certain social characteristics of the opposition movement in Petrograd that may have had a greater bearing on events than we have recognized; and by attempting, finally, to relate these characteristics to the opposition's failure in the capital to "gain the upper hand." It might then be possible to frame a broader argument by way of conclusion about the failure of labor protest generally in this period, and to gain a somewhat fuller understanding of the complex processes involved in the Bolsheviks' consolidation of power.

[2] G. Aronson, "Ouvriers russes conre le Bolchevisme," *Le Contrat social* 10(1966):202.

Long-term patterns

At the risk of emphasizing the obvious, let me stress, first, the importance of remembering that whereas the Bolsheviks came to power reflecting politically the perceived interests and will of a great number of Russia's fifteen to eighteen million workers,[3] they did so only as part of a vast social upheaval over which they had, in fact, very little control. Theirs was, to be sure, a critical part, vital of course to the *political* outcome of 1917; but equally important is the way in which the overthrow of the old order involved, simultaneously, a massive, and ultimately for the Bolsheviks, problematic assault on a wide array of social relationships and values that reflected Russia's political institutions. Authority based on traditional social hierarchies in the workplace weakened dramatically, as it did in the army and elsewhere, as the Provisional Government's political power itself began to decline. What emerged from this assault was social polarization and the civil war mentality used by Lenin and his comrades to such great political advantage. Ordinary workers and peasants developed a new understanding of the nature of "democratic Russia" that reflected elemental notions of social dominance – *vlast'* – rather than the relatively rarefied (and nonRussian) concepts of a rule of law and universal civil liberties. For our purposes, however, what needs to be stressed in this regard is not the Bolsheviks' obvious relative political strength by the fall of 1917, or their skillful arrogation of mass "democratic" commitments to further mobilize workers, but rather the party's *weakness* in facing the monumental tasks of Russia's social and economic reconstruction.

Crucial to the emergence of Lenin's new order, moreover, was a familiar range of new or newly reestablished mass organizations – factory committees, trade unions, workers' control organizations, and the like – that not only reflected workers' ideas about democracy and social change, but also represented workers' solutions to acute socioeconomic problems. Although the Bolsheviks increasingly identified with these mass organizations

---

[3] The number (and definition) of "workers" in Russia at this time is the subject of much dispute. See L. S. Gaponenko, *Rabochii klass Rossii v 1917 godu* (Moscow, 1970), 33–75, who gives 15 million as the figure for all hired labor in industry, including transport, construction, and agricultural workers, and 18.5 million for all hired labor in general (p. 75).

as the revolution unfolded, they were not primarily of the party's making, any more than was the overthrow of the tsarist regime. On the contrary, it remained quite unclear to Lenin and others in the party leadership, whose sights were focused on securing political power, exactly how these organizations or the values they reflected corresponded to the requirements of a communist order. The party's support for institutions such as factory committees was conditioned in large measure by the desire to destroy bourgeois Russia, and by the fact that many in the committee movement became Bolsheviks themselves. The further social upheaval needed to complete the assault on Russia's "bourgeois order" was, in fact, also clearly an impediment to the party's need to create the stable socioeconomic conditions required for social welfare, as well as for socialism.

At the same time, the Russian workers' movement of 1917 was itself a product of longer processes of change, including the uneven and dependent nature of Russian industrial development during the war, and the differential impact of the war itself on various industrial and social groups. Even though the period between July 1914 and the spring of 1915 brought some dislocation almost everywhere, the needs of the war soon began to have a strengthening effect on some industries. By the late spring of 1915, as state resources were mobilized to support defense production, and deferments and exemptions were introduced for skilled workers, a complex process of industrial segregation began to unfold, separating "favored" industries from those the state was unable or unwilling to protect, on the one hand, and identifying particular branches of production and particular plants for special consideration, on the other.

The broadest patterns of segregation are visible in output data. Total industrial production grew some 21.5 percent between 1913 and 1916, but this was almost entirely the result of increased output in only two sectors, metals and chemicals. In Russia's two most populous industrial branches, food processing and cotton textiles, output fell 22 percent and 18 percent, respectively, between 1913 and 1916.[4] These differential rates were at least partly attributable to the nature of government intervention. State re-

---

[4] Of the other major industrial sectors, only leather, linen, hemp and jute, and some clothing branches (including shoes) showed any increase whatsoever, and accounted for only 8.3 percent of new output. Wood production fell 38 percent, and the production of paper some 20 percent.

sources began to pour into weapons and armament production, especially in Petrograd, and into the production of gunpowder and explosives, soon the major product of chemical plants. These sectors also gained priority in fuel and resource allocations, and were the beneficiaries of new machine tool imports, financed at state expense, which helped output per worker increase some 40 percent in metals and some 30 percent in chemicals between 1915 and 1917. By contrast, output per worker fell from between 15 percent and 20 percent in almost all other sectors, and more than 30 percent in lumber mills and factories making wood products. Textiles were particularly affected.

At the same time, the state bestowed the largest and most lucrative military contracts on a relatively small number of major producers. As late as February 1917, demand for military goods from Petrograd metalworking plants was still some 16 percent greater than their production capacity, a ratio that, among other things, allowed Petrograd metalworkers the luxury of striking without great fear of massive retaliation. In chemicals, the state's demand was even higher.

These developments had important social consequences, some of which are well known: The number of metalworkers in Petrograd increased by some 400 percent between 1914 and 1917, and the number of chemical workers by 250 percent. These enormous increases, however, were accompanied by, and in part engendered, a deep instability in the workplace, even in chemicals and metals. At the Putilov works, for example, some 9,000 employees left their jobs in 1915 alone, some to the army, some to higher paying jobs elsewhere. At the Treugol'nik rubber plant in the nearby Narvskii district, the number of workers replaced in 1915 may have exceeded 10,000. If we lack precise figures on these changes, their dynamics are still clear and quite extraordinary. In Russia as a whole, at least one-third of all workers employed in January 1914 had left their jobs by 1917, and the actual figure was probably much higher. In Moscow alone more than 300,000 filed through the labor exchange during the first nine months of its operation in 1915–16.

Many newcomers to the industrial labor force were women, and their employment helped effect a decline in real wages in all industrial sectors. More important for our purposes, however, is the likelihood that these changes contributed to the ero-

sion of the relative security of skilled workers, both in terms of
real wages, and as a result of the introduction of new machinery,
new factory discipline, and the further rationalization of work
processes.[5] These developments took place against a background of rising living costs, growing shortages of food and other
essentials, and increasing labor militancy, particularly in Petrograd. Manufacturers and the government responded in many
places with arrests, dismissals, fines, and such tactics as compul-
sory overtime, which added greatly to the burdens of maintaining some semblance of family stability or welfare.

It is important, finally, to emphasize even in bare outline some
of the ways in which all of these processes related to Russia's
revolutionary development in 1917, and helped define the problems that Lenin and his comrades might be said to have inherited as they came to power in October. Not least among these is
the way in which many workers heralded February as the op-
portunity, at long last, to establish some degree of stability and
order in the workplace, in part by ending arbitrary and repressive behavior of managers and foremen, in part by assuring steady
and orderly production with adequate wages and secure jobs.
Undoubtedly skilled workers and artisans felt strongly the desire
for security, hoping to maintain the traditional perquisites of
their crafts; but semiskilled machine operators and even unskilled workers, who must have looked with some envy at their
better paid and more secure comrades, clearly felt the same desire. In any event, the important points are that the quest for
security was very broadly based; that it accompanied more familiar expectations for an improvement in material welfare in
1917 (reflected, for example, in the wage and hour demands of
strikers in the spring); and that both sets of aspirations accompanied from the start more politicized hopes for the creation of
a democratic order.

Yet one of the most salient aspects of 1917 was the inability of
the Provisional Government not only to stem the processes of
economic deterioration throughout the country as a whole, but
even to prevent its spread into "favored" industrial sectors. Most

---

[5] See the discussion in Heather Hogan, "Industrial Rationalization and the Roots
of Labor Militance in the St. Petersburg Metalworking Industry, 1901–1914,"
Russian Review 42(1983):163–90.

important, defense production itself fell by as much as 40 percent between February and July; and output from all metalworking and machine plants declined by almost a third from
1916. Coal production in the Donbas, which had been as much
as 172 million puds [1 pud = 36 lb.] as late as November 1916
and which was crucial to iron and steel production, fell to less
than 110 million puds by the end of the summer. Reserves await-
ing shipment at mine heads were only one-fifth of what they had
been in 1916. By early 1917, many plants, like the Parviainen
works in Petrograd, had less than a single day's reserve of coal.
Putilov, which used some 10 percent of all industrial coal deliv-
eries in the capital, by mid-August was receiving only one-quarter
of what it needed.

If by late summer 1917, therefore, "crisis" had become a common noun in all Russian public discourse, one must especially
appreciate the ways in which the country's threatened economic
collapse now raised the specter of massive hardship and ruina-
tion even for "privileged" workers in the Petrograd metal plants.
Russia's economy seemed threatened with systemic collapse.
Central financial institutions like the stock exchanges began to
weaken, along with the various regulatory agencies governing
commodity exchange. The normative processes of capitalist finance – investments, loans, issuing stocks and bonds, collecting
receivables, the repayment of debt – were all seriously disrupted
by the summer of 1917. Risks increased drastically. The state
banking apparatus came under tremendous pressure.

What must be emphasized is that these circumstances seemed
to many to require energetic state intervention at precisely the
moment the Provisional Government itself was under increasing
attack from all sides, and mortally weak. It is important concep-
tually, as it was important tactically for Lenin and other activists
at the time, to distinguish "state" and "government" in this regard. The government, clearly, was ineffective. Increasingly, this
seemed due to the ways that it reflected "bourgeois" interests.
The state apparatus itself, however, still seemed to afford workers at least the *possibility* of economic and social relief, especially
with the formation of the first coalition in May, and then again,
after July, when the Soviet's declaration of July 8 became, in
effect, the platform of the second coalition. Countless workers' delegations besieged state offices throughout this period de-

manding assistance, even as the "bourgeois" ministers themselves came under increasing attack. And if from the standpoint of democratic politics one can understand the Provisional Government's reluctance to have the state intervene further in the economy, one can also understand why growing numbers of workers came to see the Provisional regime as reflecting, above all, the failures and insecurities of "bourgeois capitalism."

It is against the background of these broader processes that one must appreciate the enormous impact of more immediate changes, both before and after October, and understand important aspects of the workers' own response. And here one must note not only the problems associated with the formation of factory committees and other autonomous workers' organizations, but the related emergence of two broad tendencies among workers that also had a bearing on events, and that were, in important ways, contradictory. There emerged on the one hand, as S. A. Smith has argued convincingly,[6] a forceful and increasingly strident sense of proletarian class identity – a generalized class consciousness that reflected broad patterns of social polarization – that was of crucial political importance, and served so vital a role in the Bolsheviks coming to power. On the other hand, however, there also emerged a somewhat less familiar but equally important concurrent tendency toward what one might call "localism," in which traditionally unifying national loyalties and commitments gave way to concerns bounded by factory gates. The developing characteristics of proletarian and peasant social hegemony increasingly were defined in terms of particularistic (rather than class) interests and needs. Localism was at once a natural result of the need workers felt to find immediate "solutions" in 1917 to the problems of their own plants and factories, and the result of longer-term social influences – craft identities and consciousness, common backgrounds (*zemliachestvo*), and the like.[7]

As Russia's crisis deepened and class-conscious workers in-

[6] S. A. Smith, "Craft Consciousness, Class Consciousness: Petrograd 1917," *History Workshop Journal* 11(Spring 1981):33–58. See also William G. Rosenberg, "Workers and Workers' Control in the Russian Revolution," *History Workshop Journal* 5(Spring 1978):89–97.
[7] See, for example, James D. White, "The Sormovo-Nikolaev zemlyachestvo in the February Revolution," *Soviet Studies* 31(1979):475–504.

creasingly took local matters into their own hands, the defensive (and particularistic) functions of factory committees took on increasing importance. Moreover, and especially important to events after October, the strongest and most active factory committees emerged in Russia's favored and most protected industrial branches and plants. More than half the delegates at the first conference of factory committees in Petrograd in late May and early June, for example, were from the capital's metalworking plants. They represented more than 230,000 workers in 134 enterprises, and as an industrial group constituted a delegation eight times larger than both the printers (the next most heavily represented branch) and the textile workers. By August 1917, at the second Petrograd conference, chemical workers constituted the second largest delegation, and by now had almost three times as many representatives as the printers.

It is important to emphasize the obvious political aspects of this process. As Smith demonstrates in *Red Petrograd,* factory committees played out within an enterprise the broader struggle for control over resources and the distribution of power. At the same time, both moderate Soviet leaders and Provisional Government figures could not fail to incur workers' animosity as they tried to restrain the committees' growing influence. When socialist Minister of Labor M. I. Skobelev tried late in the summer to set limits on committee power, workers responded by saying, "Precisely now, when disruption of the economy is reaching new heights, when firings have become massive and factories all over the place are being closed and evacuated, the intensive, unrestricted and most diverse work of factory committees and their central organs is absolutely necessary." In fact, of course, not only were all such workers' groups powerless to stem the systemic disintegration of Russia's state capitalist economy in 1917, but indeed they made matters worse. More important in terms of developments after October, they also increased by their actions an overall dependency on state, as opposed to market, economic mechanisms.

It is at least partly against this background that the Bolsheviks soon appeared so attractive to many Russian workers in 1917, especially in Petrograd. Lenin and his comrades offered both an explanation for Russia's crisis, and the simultaneous hope that complete disaster could be avoided if government authorities used the country's seemingly vast state resources in the workers' own interests. Thus the Bolsheviks' own arguments about the relationship between the war and capitalism generally, their insistence that Russia's threatened economic collapse could be attributed largely to industrialists "sabotaging" the revolution in order to preserve social and political hegemony, and above all, their emphasis on seizing state power and using it to "smash the capitalist order" all seemed both to explain Russia's crisis and to promise effective, permanent solutions – all the more, in fact, because they involved at least some elements of truth. Russia's particular form of capitalism *was* failing, as a system of finance, commodity exchange, social relations, and industrial production; indeed, it had already begun to fail before February, a process at once the cause and consequence of political weakness, social upheaval, and the carnage of war. Little wonder thousands of workers with varying degrees of political consciousness regarded so enthusiastically the "overthrow of capitalism and the end of the bourgeois order," and anticipated so hopefully an end to the insecurities of liberal democracy.

Social characteristics of the opposition movement

One of the most salient features of revolutionary Russia in the eight months or so after October 1917 is that nothing seemed to have changed for the better. This realization, and the even more precarious, uncertain conditions that soon emerged, disturbed and angered broad groups of workers. By the early summer there were widespread anti-Bolshevik protests. Armed clashes occurred in the factory districts of Petrograd and other industrial centers. Under the aegis of the Conference of Factory and Plant Representatives (*Sobranie Upolnomochennykh Fabrik i Zavodov Petrograda*), a general strike was set for July 2.

In October most celebrating workers did not suspect that this would be the short-term outcome of one of the most momentous changes in Russian history. For a few short weeks, while capitalist management began to disappear from their factories, workers seemed to believe that they themselves could find at least temporary solutions to the problems besetting their plants, and that Bolshevik rule would assist these efforts, both by using the state apparatus in their support, especially in the area of banking and finance, and by restoring some semblance of economic control. By early December, encouraged by the Bolsheviks' draft decree promising the "legal" extension of workers' control in all enterprises with more than five employees, workers had organized committees in more than 2,100 major enterprises, including some 68 percent of all plants with more than 200 workers. Scores of plants and major railroads were "nationalized" from below in the expectation that this would finally guarantee effective state assistance. "What had begun to happen before the October Revolution now happened more frequently and more openly," E. H. Carr writes of this process. "For the moment, nothing would have dammed the tide of revolt."[8]

But it is doubtful that the principal force behind the "tide of revolt" after October was essentially a political one, and even unlikely that many Bolsheviks were primarily concerned with workers' control in order "to secure the allegiance of the working masses," as Paul Avrich has suggested.[9] The consolidation of power was clearly the central concern of Lenin and his comrades, and the factory committee movement was obviously of political importance, but what occurred in November and early December was not so much revolt (or perhaps, more precisely, not only revolt) as an effort by workers to stave off total economic disaster on a local level by securing a dominant role in plant affairs. In political terms, the revolt was largely over. State power, such as it was, belonged to workers' parties, even if not yet to the Bolsheviks alone. The enormously difficult and frightening task now was to cope with production problems and survive, a task that workers simply could no longer leave to others, and for which now, more than ever, they needed state support.

The very necessity of this process further strengthened the defensive characteristics of factory committees in these weeks. November and December 1917 were months in which factory committees desperately sought new orders for goods, had to

---

[8] E. H. Carr, *The Bolshevik Revolution, 1917–1923*, 3 vols. (New York: Macmillan, 1950–3), 2:69.

[9] Paul H. Avrich, "The Bolshevik Revolution and Workers' Control in Russian Industry," *Slavic Review* 22(1963):48.

procure scarce materials and supplies, turn up funds to pay workers, and resolve their own difficulties with technicians and other experienced administrators in order to keep plants running. In many places managers and workers' representatives signed papers together in order to receive funds (especially from private banks) or procure goods. Elsewhere, seats on factory committees were given to technicians to prevent their departure and assure their help. Collegial administration emerged as a common form of management, in other words, because it seemed the most effective way to get things done. Meanwhile, committees explained their actions at frequent meetings and sought popular confirmation for their policies through "plant democracy."

Moreover, for a period perhaps no longer than six to eight weeks, many in the factories must have thought these efforts were working. Taking control of production in many enterprises gave committees immediate access to financial reserves and other resources remaining in the commercial "pipeline." Some new funds thus became available for the moment for pay increases, procuring materials, even settling outstanding obligations in cases where suppliers demanded immediate payment. Private wealth, of course, was also confiscated, and in many places redistributed to workers along with space in apartments and other sequestered living quarters. Workers entered their plants in early November with a new sense of commitment and enthusiasm, convinced their insecurity and dislocation would soon come to an end. Russian workers were buoyed by a political triumph that wrested state power from the bourgeoisie, confident in their own ability to manage affairs, and elated by the reality of their new social dominance. Workers could hardly fail to expect that conditions would improve as their leaders and comrades within the Bolshevik party now began to employ the full resources of the state in support of their own class interests.

Irreversible forces were already working to pulverize these hopes, of course, and to destroy even a semblance of economic order. The very process of draining the pipeline for immediate gain made ultimate disaster inevitable unless the flow of goods could be increased at their source. Solving this problem required the total reconstruction of Russia's economic infrastructure, a task difficult enough in any circumstance, but now almost impossible in the time required to maintain the supply of goods and materials needed to keep most plants in operation. It also became clear that little effective assistance would be forthcoming from various state agencies, even for nationalized plants. Despite taking over state banks and other agencies, the Bolsheviks were simply not able to provide the relief workers expected, and whose promise was implicit in the party coming to power.

Quite to the contrary, in fact. The very seizure of state power contributed enormously – if indirectly – to undermining workers' material well-being by precipitating one of the most rapid and least controlled military demobilizations in history, a process that had begun before October, of course, but that now erupted without restraint. The more familiar side of demobilization involved the breakup of the old army: Within weeks hundreds of thousands had left their units, armed, impatient, often angry. But demobilization meant as well the reorientation of industry from war to peacetime needs, an overwhelming task even in conditions of relative political stability. In Petrograd more than 70 percent of all Russian industrial production was directed toward military needs; some 80 percent of the industrial workforce was in defense-related occupations. As late as September 1917 there were also some seven million men still in uniform. As the Bolsheviks pursued their peace plans and the army dissolved, most state procurements ceased. In some places, manufacturers stopped production in mid-stream. Elsewhere, payments were not made when goods were ready in early November.

Delegations of anxious workers pressured Soviet and state officials alike for relief as difficulties mounted, but the magnitude of the problem was simply overwhelming. The Council of People's Commissars of the new soviet regime itself may have made matters worse by decreeing in December that strictly military production should cease entirely ("for example, work on artillery shells"), an order that sent shock waves through plants like the Petrograd Trubochnyi works, Russia's largest producer in 1917 of shell casings. Factory committees and unions were simply to "take the most decisive measures to find work" for displaced workers, "sending delegations to the Urals, to the north, and so forth, in order to work out necessary arrangements."

Late December and early January thus saw a transition in proletarian Russia from relative enthusiasm and even some limited material improvement to extremely rapid economic decline, deepening insecurity, and in some places outright panic. Petrograd, the very center of proletarian power, with its heavy concentration of armament and other defense industries, suffered most. Between January and April 1918, the supply of goods coming into the capital dropped precipitously in almost every category.[10] Almost 60 percent of the industrial workforce here was forced into the streets.

Aggregate figures are less important for our purposes, however, than the distribution of unemployed workers by industrial branch in Petrograd. And what is most striking is not simply the extent of the crisis, but its unevenness and the singular concentration of unemployed workers in what had been Russia's most favored industries and plants. The greatest declines by far were in chemicals (including rubber) and metals, 79 percent and 74 percent, respectively, in April 1918, relative to January 1917. These two branches, moreover, had employed by far the greatest number of workers in Petrograd before October, some 250,000 (more than 70 percent), excluding those in service occupations. Hence the spring of 1918 saw the emergence of an extraordinary concentration of unemployed workers in what had been the city's best paid, most numerous, and most secure section of the workforce, employed in the largest and most productive plants.

In contrast, Petrograd textile workers, who had suffered severe dislocation during the first years of the war, as we have seen, now suffered only a 15 percent decline (21 percent if one includes the 5,000 or so workers who had been employed in cotton cloth manufacturing, and where production was now further curtailed because cotton imports were shut off). Leather workers declined 31 percent; food workers, 23 percent; and paper manufacturing, 22 percent.

The Bolsheviks' decision to evacuate Petrograd clearly con-

---

[10] Carloads of cattle, meat, and fowl dropped more than 85 percent; eggs by 90 percent; sugar and salt by more than 70 percent; similarly with fuel oil, peat, and coal. From an average of some 4.8 million puds of coal per month in 1917, a figure that was already only half of what it had been in 1916, Petrograd received an average of only 0.9 million puds a month in early 1918, and only 0.5 million puds of oil, one-quarter of the city's monthly average for 1917. The declines in other goods were comparable.

tributed to the crisis. Information here is obviously incomplete, and the process itself was chaotic. Even so, it seems clear that the largest group of out-migrants was not, as one might suspect, skilled workers being transferred to industrial centers elsewhere in the country, but unskilled labor and recent in-migrants. Even allowing for errors in the records, it seems likely that a very large proportion of unemployed workers remaining in the capital were skilled and semiskilled metalworkers and defense workers – the very social group who had enjoyed such relative prosperity before February and had constituted one of the Bolsheviks' strongest bases of support in the capital throughout 1917, and whose revolutionary expectations had been raised the highest.

While the magnitude of the crisis in both objective and subjective terms is hard to measure, it is also difficult to underestimate. So is the suddenness with which the crisis undercut workers' hopes. February and March 1918 were months of precarious uncertainty. Factories that stayed open were unable to get new orders for goods, supplies and materials dwindled, funds dried up, pilfering and theft were common, and decrees from the center were "almost totally ignored." Productivity, of course, fell precipitously. The more mechanized a plant (and thus the higher its complement of skilled and semiskilled workers), the greater the problems of maintaining production, given the lack of fuel and spare parts.[11] It is hardly surprising in these circumstances that some workers sold off machinery and equipment, acts ridiculed by observers as brainless anarchism.

What is important for our purposes, however, is not so much the magnitude of this disaster in statistical terms as the ways in which it may have acted quickly to undermine workers' confidence and sense of unity, and given new impetus to centrifugal tendencies that had largely been overcome in the fall. Questions of worker unity and the broad issues of power were now largely past, partly because many activists were themselves siphoned away from the factories, partly because, as one Bolshevik observer put it, political questions per se were no longer urgent with workers

---

[11] Peat production in the Central Industrial Region, for example, accounting for some 70 percent of the country's total output, fell to near zero precisely because less than 3 percent was still produced by hand, and workers were unable to keep equipment running.

and Bolsheviks in power. What mattered instead was how to get help "from above," and how to manage individual factories, a situation that put enormous pressure on workers' committees. It was now the committees' responsibility alone, for example, even in plants still under private ownership, to decide what to do with demobilized soldiers appearing at their gates and demanding their old jobs back; and it was logically the committees who now assumed responsibility for regulating wages and imposing plant discipline – or, as V. Maiskii put it in April, for finding "disciplinary measures . . . which appeal not to the best, but to the worst side of human nature, not to revolutionary enthusiasm, but to direct self-interest." One historian has described committee activities at this time as "bringing Russia to the brink of economic collapse."[12] But more to the point is the way in which committees were forced to assume extensive new responsibilities and powers at precisely the moment they could least effectively meet them, and when any action whatsoever on their part was bound to create dissension. In contrast to 1917, moreover, the "bourgeoisie" was now a much less ready target for worker dissidence. The familiar cry of 1917 that the government was defending "capitalist" interests could no longer explain the lack of effective state intervention.

Particularly heavy tasks fell on committees in plants formerly tied to military production; and where a shift had been made to natural wages, committees could never satisfy demand.[13] Frequently delivery of wages required the use of armed force, although there were many other reasons as well why committees built their militias in these weeks. Goods needed protection, committee meetings were often disrupted, and attacks on warehouses, storage sheds, even rail lines began to occur almost daily. Clashes between groups from different factories also became more frequent as conditions deteriorated. Even dormitories were invaded; and as factory militias tightened their control at plant

---

[12] Avrich, "Bolshevik Revolution," 58.
[13] With the publication of the decree on demobilization the Erikson telephone factory suddenly found all its outstanding military orders canceled outright, and had to ask for "voluntary resignations" until new buyers could be found. Workers responded by demanding six weeks' terminal wages, and in the face of their anger the factory committee yielded, even though this meant all work would soon have to stop.

gates, employment documents came to matter as much as ration cards.

In these circumstances the reemergence of both craft consciousness and factory particularism was inevitable. If maintaining a job in a particular shop or factory became one's primary source of security, local commitments naturally had to increase. The tasks that now seemed most urgent in personal and practical terms were simply not conducive to sustaining broader allegiances, especially since the principal goal for which workers had mobilized in 1917 – the overthrow of capitalism and the creation of a "workers' state" – had now been achieved. In the spring of 1918 one's occupation again came to matter significantly *for workers as well as for others*, and in ways hardly conducive to harmonious social relations even within factory gates.

Evidence is skimpy, and one can only hypothesize about the degree of real conflict that emerged on these grounds, but both the available evidence and the logic of events themselves press in this direction. Facing impossible tasks, unable to meet workers' needs and demands, and now in some places working closely with technical personnel or even former factory administrators, the committees themselves increasingly became the objects of workers' anger, even as (and in fact, precisely because) their powers were increasing. Workers at the Nobel factory (chemicals), Old Lessner (metal processing), and the Okhtenskii powder works (chemicals) turned sharply against their own factory committees in late January and February for "excessive discipline" and "inadequate administration": Those "privileged" to sit on committees were now acting "too much like factory administrators," even "carrying out their orders" and "defending employer interests, not ours." "Comrades elect their factory committee and within a week the grumbling begins." New factory meetings are called, new instructions issued from the workers, and soon "the cycle begins again." Such antagonism, moreover, logically ran both ways, since from the committee members' viewpoint, rank-and-file hostility was hardly fair. It was also a genuine threat to plant operations and led to new demands for discipline, often accompanied by charges of laziness and irresponsibility. Events were coming full circle, back to the very issues of concern and protest that had surfaced in the spring of 1917, except that now they occurred under Bolshevik rule and were thus necessarily focused on the workers' own representatives.

One must emphasize the contradictory nature of these pressures in the late winter of 1918, and appreciate as well the manner in which they simultaneously reinforced a commitment to collegiality and democracy within many enterprises, a desire for autonomy, and at the same time, reinforced social tensions and demands for effective state intervention. Autonomy was necessary because factories everywhere needed to protect themselves from the "paroxysm of requisitioning taking hold of all official agencies," as leather workers expressed it. Effective state intervention remained necessary because of the overwhelming need for orders, goods, and essential supplies. Plant democracy, finally, was essential not only because of workers' own political commitments and values, but also because factory committees themselves recognized that "rank-and-file confidence" was critical to sustaining production, as the chairman of the Nikolaev railroad committee put it, and that complex production problems simply were not amenable to any other form of management on a local level. The trust and cooperation of those they represented, in fact, were the committees' best hope for maintaining any production whatsoever.

Bolsheviks and workers after October

Lenin's approach to these issues is familiar: Economic chaos was fundamentally the consequence of prerevolutionary circumstances; the factory committee movement reflected dangerous anarchistic and syndicalistic tendencies, as it had even in 1917, despite its importance as a political base for the party; factory administration had to come under the centralizing and coordinating control of trade unions, which themselves had to be integrated into the Bolsheviks' state and party apparatus. Almost without exception, spokesmen for the various chief committees and commissions set up within the new structure of the Council of People's Commissars condemned the autonomy and independence of factory or railroad committees and assailed workers for lack of discipline. "There are no collegial administrations anywhere in the world like ours," a prominent Bolshevik authority on the railroads complained, "where the majority of members are switchmen, engineers, and other rank-and-file employees." N. Osinskii (V. V. Obolenskii), head of the Supreme Economic Council, described workers' control as a form of "disintegrative syndicalism"; trade unionists like A. Lozovskii demanded that committees be restrained. On March 23 the Council of People's Commissars issued a decree "On the Centralization of Railroad Administration," placing "dictatorial power" in the hands of a single person in each administrative center, and thereby making clear its future plans for industrial management everywhere.

Yet it was just this confidence in the efficacy of one-man management that startled committee members themselves. From below, it simply did not seem that most plants and enterprises could be managed in this way. "If it were only the case that a dictatorship would improve matters," workers discussing the March 23 decree insisted, "the question of what to do would be clear. But . . . we've heard these songs sung for years. In the past, these 'iron hands' brought nothing but trouble."

Indeed, it seems apparent that many workers themselves, particularly in Petrograd, had now come to believe, just as earlier, that confusion and anarchy *at the top* were the major causes of their difficulties, and with some justification. The fact was that Bolshevik administration was chaotic. An endless series of miscalculations occurred in these weeks. Scores of competitive and conflicting Bolshevik and Soviet authorities issued contradictory orders, often brought to factories by armed Chekists. The Supreme Economic Council itself operated from Osinskii's suite in the Astoria hotel, issuing dozens of orders and passing countless directives with virtually no real knowledge of affairs. Scores of technicians were dismissed *from above* in this way, despite the insistence of workers' committees that the technicians' skills were crucial to operations, and the view of some officials, like the Commissar of Transport, that this was "absolutely wrong." Demobilization, as we have seen, was unplanned; the evacuation of Petrograd was chaotic. The greater the authority of the center in these weeks, the more factories like the Parviainen works found their own supplies requisitioned.[14] "Accusations of 'anarcho-

---

[14] The Treugol'nik works, for example, shut its doors after a special delegation sent to Rostov brought back forty tank cars of fuel, only to have them requisitioned by the Council of People's Commissars.

syndicalism' have always come in Russia from anti-worker, right-wing elements," one railroad committee spokesman put it; "how very strange that representatives of Bolshevik power now join in similar denunciations."

Thus, after the initial weeks of "triumph" and the period of traumatic demobilization and rapid socioeconomic decline in the winter, a third stage began to unfold in the evolution of Bolshevik labor relations after October, one that soon led to open conflict, repression, and the consolidation of Bolshevik dictatorship over the proletariat in place of proletarian dictatorship itself. Brest Litovsk was clearly a turning point, in Petrograd and elsewhere. If we can judge from newspapers like *Petrogradskoe Ekho*, a reasonably objective nonparty evening daily, even to state workers at the Tula armament works the peace treaty seemed "treasonous, ... destructive to the international proletarian movement, and deeply harmful to the interests of Russian workers, the revolution, and the Russian economy in general." There were also feelings of panic in the capital that the peace would not hold, and that Germans would soon enter the city. Groups of Putilov workers demanded immediate payment of one-and-one-half months' wages, insisting that soviet power was *their* power, and the demands of the lower orders had to be met.

It is hardly surprising that worker opposition to the Bolsheviks also became much more visible in these weeks, partly organized around the Conference of Factory and Plant Representatives in Petrograd and Moscow. A major outbreak of worker protest in Petrograd occurred around the closing of the Constituent Assembly, when a number of demonstrators were killed and wounded. Thousands had gathered at the Obukhov works in the southeastern district of the city and at nearby plants in the Nevskii district, including the important Aleksandrovsk locomotive works. There were also protests at several plants in the Vyborg district, and at the Trubochnyi works on Vasil'evskii Island.[15]

Undoubtedly Socialist Revolutionary and Menshevik activists stirred up some of this protest. The Obukhov works was known as an SR stronghold, and there was clearly still considerable support for both parties, particularly their left faction, throughout

---

[15] According to Bolshevik accounts some twenty-one persons were killed, but the number was undoubtedly higher.

the city. Yet in some ways, these protests seemed more to mark the diffusion and even irrelevance of organized party politics at this juncture. Speakers denounced the shootings, attacking the Council of People's Commissars and the Petrograd Soviet, and expressed outrage at the closing of the Assembly. But the greatest shock seemed to be over the brutality with which Bolshevik forces had turned "on their own." The protests also centered in major state enterprises engaged in war production and directly affected by demobilization. Thus the deteriorating social circumstances of "favored" workers in proletarian Petrograd may well have begun to eclipse the issues of politics per se, while the Bolsheviks' own condemnation of the shootings and their courage in addressing angry workers (particularly at Obukhov, which had suffered a major share of the casualties) tended to depoliticize workers' anger. In any event, in the aftermath of the Assembly's closing, many in Petrograd seem to have become genuinely indifferent to the struggles and fate of other parties as political organizations, as if they belonged to the days before October.

It is largely in this context that one needs to understand the emergence of the Conference of Factory and Plant Representatives as a center of worker dissidence. In mid-January a meeting described in the press as a "Workers' Conference of the Union to Defend the Constituent Assembly" took place in Petrograd, organized in the main, apparently, by self-described "Right" Mensheviks disaffected from their Central Committee over the question of cooperation with the Bolsheviks. They were determined to build a new, representative movement "from below," shedding formal party affiliations. Workers from a number of plants soon joined them in forming the conference as a broad-based assembly, hoping among other things to counter what one observer lamented as the Petrograd workers' new "passivity and indifference." The first "extraordinary" meeting of the conference convened in Petrograd on March 13 in the midst of new protests over the evacuation, which occurred most intensely just before Brest Litovsk when it seemed the city might fall under German control.[16]

---

[16] At Putilov anxious workers demanded information from the Metalworkers' Union about evacuation plans. Union leaders had no satisfactory answers, but castigated workers in turn for meeting during working hours. At the Westinghouse plant workers sent an angry delegation to the city soviet with similar

Delegates attended from at least fifteen major metalworking plants, including the Obukhov, Trubochnyi, and Aleksandrovsk mechanical plants, which were scenes of protest in January, and a number of print shops, which were, of course, Menshevik strongholds. The delegates' mood was angry, and focused directly on those seemingly responsible for the "chaos of evacuation," shortages of food and other goods, and the arbitrary exercise of authority, but the delegates were also confused and desperate. "The workers are lost," a spokesman from the Rechkin plant declared; "it seems to them that everything is falling apart."

Reports of the March 13 conference appeared in Social Democratic newspapers as well as in what remained of the nonparty press. On April 7 the Menshevik Central Committee officially endorsed the conference, yielding to the Right Menshevik conception of "appealing broadly to workers' gatherings in order to facilitate the formation of working-class consciousness and reconstructing labor unity," or, as M. I. Liber put it at a Moscow committee plenum one week later, allowing workers to feel "the strength of their class position." By this time there were apparently representatives in more than forty Petrograd enterprises, officially "representing," if that is the proper term, some 55,000 or more workers. Five meetings were reportedly held between March 13 and the end of the month. According to an account published in *Den'*, 33 of the 110 participants at the March 13 meeting were Socialist Revolutionaries, 35 were Social Democrats (Unityists), one was a Popular Socialist, and 42 were nonparty. On April 3 a second "extraordinary" meeting took place where the Bolsheviks were attacked directly for "assaulting the workers' movement with tsarist methods."

What is important in all this, however, is not only the weakening of Bolshevik support, but also the powerful, contradictory pressures building from below in the spring of 1918 for solutions to problems that, at the time, were essentially insoluble. What seems most striking about the disaffection that the conference demonstrated is the focus on the breakdown of order, disillusionment with revolutionary politics generally (party affilia-

---

questions. To the question "Where do we go?" soviet spokesmen are reported to have told them, "wherever you like," suggesting that they take "whatever they like" with them!

tions notwithstanding), and the insistence on a greater degree of local plant autonomy, despite overt hostility toward plant administrators and the delegates' own factory committees. Conference delegates attacked not only the Bolsheviks, but also the soviets "which have ceased to be the political representatives of the proletariat and are little more than judicial or police institutions." They condemned the Red Guards for their brutality, but demanded more protection for their dormitories and factories, and asserted their own right to use force. They demanded freer trade regulations, following their Menshevik and Socialist Revolutionary leaders, an end to restrictions on movement, and also insisted on the right to manage their own affairs, while bitterly attacking trade unions and their own factory committees for "not fulfilling their obligations to the workers":

The war has ended but our misfortunes are only beginning. There is little work; a senseless, disorderly evacuation has virtually destroyed industry. Workers are being thrown out on the streets by the tens of thousands. It is impossible to go anywhere, and there is nowhere to go. Our last coins are being spent. A hungry summer is coming. We cannot expect help from anyone. Are the trade unions doing much for the unemployed? They aren't concerned with the unemployed, and aren't even concerned with the employed. The unions organize the economy, not the workers. Factory committees organize commissions to fire workers, organize bureaucratic organs which don't need our trust and have long lost it. And they don't help us.

There were strong overtones here as well of rank-and-file hostility to the more privileged workers who now may have controlled many factory committees, and whose factory positions, in any event, were more secure. In the view of many, an "irresponsible technical apparatus" was now in charge of many factories, falsely representing rank-and-file interest: "[Our committees] ought immediately to refuse to do the things that are not properly their real tasks, sever their links with the government, and become organs of the free will of the working class, organs of its struggle." "We state honestly and openly that we have lost all faith in those above us." These views, moreover, were no less strident for the fact that those "above" them, in committees and unions, were also struggling with authorities in almost precisely the same terms, as we have seen, and being condemned in return for anarchism and acts "contrary to proletarian state interests."

Obviously the generalized (and to some extent, internally contradictory) protest was partly the result of the efforts of Socialist Revolutionary and Menshevik activists. But evidence on the social composition of conference delegates indicates that the protest was also related more acutely to Petrograd's critical socioeconomic circumstances. In effect, only two major industrial branches – printing and metalworking – were represented in conference meetings, and the largest number of "delegates" (the nature of actual representation remains an open question) was from twenty-six metalworking plants formerly engaged in defense production, including seven that had been entirely shut down. Otherwise, the only other significant representation came from some sixteen typographers and print shops, strongholds of Menshevism. Only three of the city's food processing plants sent delegates, all from the Rozhdestvenskii district, and only two delegates represented workers in wood crafts or manufacturing. Most striking is the almost complete absence of textile workers. The one exception was the Tornton (Thornton) plant in the Vyborg district, where approximately one-third of all the factories "represented" in the conference were located.

Employment statistics help explain the textile workers' absence. For the twenty-eight factories with delegates in the conference for which we have data, the average unemployment rate on April 1, 1918 (contrasted with January 1, 1917) was 50.5 percent. In contrast, the average unemployment rate for some thirty-six major nonparticipating factories for which we have data was only 21.6 percent. The Skorokhod leather works, for example, which did not send delegates to the conference, had almost the same number of workers employed in April 1918 as it had had in January 1917 (4,900). The Bodganov works (11,669) had a similar experience, and the Laferm tobacco works actually showed an employment increase from 2,363 to 2,507. Most importantly, the relatively small employment declines we have noted among Petrograd textile workers affected primarily those working in smaller shops; employment in larger plants, which had experienced their "shake out" many months earlier, held rather steady. Thus, the Nevskii cotton plant continued to employ more than 1,700 workers in April 1918, compared to 2,056 in January 1917; the Kersten plant in Vyborg, 1,070 compared to 2,252; and the Sampsonievskaia works, also in Vyborg, 1,618 compared to 1,592 in January 1917. Although other factors also undoubtedly affected workers' connections with the Conference of Factory and Plant Representatives, the importance of social circumstances seems to have been paramount.

It is possible, albeit deductively, to get an additional fix on conference participants by taking into account the patterns of evacuation from Petrograd, and the general content of discussions at conference meetings. The animosity shown toward factory committees makes it unlikely that conference leaders were closely tied to workers' control organizations or the unions. Also, most of the skeleton crews that continued to work even at plants that had closed, tended to be, in the main, skilled workers and technical personnel. Finally, as we have noted, the least skilled laborers in the metal plants constituted the largest group of evacuees, whereas the most recent arrivals to the city, those with the closest ties to the countryside, were also the largest category of workers to leave voluntarily. We can thus deduce that the largest group of conference supporters were most probably semiskilled workers who had moved into important jobs with the great increase in military production during the war, but who now found their hopes for security and advancement crushed by an economic collapse that left them vulnerable and expendable.

The only other significant group of conference delegates, the printers, undoubtedly came in part because of their close association with the Mensheviks, but also, in all likelihood, because of the specific threat Bolshevism represented to the livelihood of what had become in 1917 one of the city's most rapidly growing industrial sectors. Thus they may well have been pushed toward the conference by social circumstances they shared, or felt they were about to share, with the metalworkers, as well as by political convictions.

By April 1918 a range of dissidence had thus emerged in Petrograd, reinforced by – and doubtlessly also reinforcing – the various forms of craft and factory particularism that had become so important in conditions of social dislocation and economic disaster. All dissident elements, from the overworked and harassed factory committees to the idle and anxious unemployed, demanded effective state intervention, particularly in Petrograd in the matter of evacuation, but elsewhere as well. Among many there was also an abhorrence of Bolshevik political repression and arbitrariness, as well as varying degrees of sympathy for the oppositional parties. The question for conference leaders was whether these various strains could be effectively mobilized.

On May 9, 1918 at the town of Kolpino near Petrograd, armed guards opened fire on an angry group of workers protesting at the local soviet over shortages of jobs and food. Word of the shooting spread quickly, and while the incident was hardly the first of its kind, it triggered a massive wave of indignation.[17] The Conference of Factory and Plant Representatives met to demand "the complete liquidation of the current regime." Work temporarily stopped at a number of plants.

Popular outrage spread rapidly. Like the Lena shootings in 1912, Kolpino quickly emerged as a focal point for more generalized anger and frustration. In Moscow, Tula, Kolomna, Nizhnii-Novgorod, Rybinsk, Orel, Tver', and elsewhere, workers gathered to issue new protests, in some cases identifying themselves openly with the conference. "The suffering of the masses has reached an extreme limit," one group insisted; "to live like this any longer is absolutely impossible." In Petrograd, textile workers went on strike for increased food rations, and a wave of demonstrations spread in response to still more Bolshevik arrests until, at the end of May, a long meeting of the conference asked workers to postpone further protests "until a more favorable moment," when better organization and coordination could lead to a citywide, and perhaps nationwide, general strike.

It is possible to trace quickly this first major wave of labor protest through to its climax in early July, and to understand, finally, its various dimensions. Contemporary newspapers and journals document more than seventy different incidents in Petrograd between Kolpino and the beginning of July, including strikes, demonstrations, and anti-Bolshevik factory meetings. Some of these were meetings convened in conjunction with Petrograd soviet elections held at the end of June. Others were less focused, sometimes addressed by speakers from various oppositional parties, sometimes not. Of the latter sort, the greatest

---

[17] Protests centered at Putilov, Siemens-Schuckert, Rechkin, and especially Obukhov, which sent a delegation to visit additional factories and mobilize further protests. On May 11 and 12 thousands gathered at meetings in the Narvskii and Nevskii districts and on Vasil'evskii Island. Some twenty-one factories sent delegations to attend the victims' funeral.

number by far were protests against some form of Bolshevik repression: shootings, incidents of "terroristic activities," and arrests. In some forty incidents workers' protests focused on these issues, and the data surely understate the actual number by a wide margin. There were as well some eighteen separate strikes or other work stoppages with an explicitly anti-Bolshevik character.

Many of the protests included calls for democratic political reforms. Seven large gatherings in May passed resolutions demanding that the Constituent Assembly be reconvened, following the program of the conference. There were an additional four meetings, only one of which seems to have been attended primarily by printers, where workers specifically demanded freedom of the press. Very few protests, in fact, appear directly related to essentially social issues: unemployment, the cost of living, and wages. Of these, most were strikes and protests over food shortages of the sort that triggered the Kolpino incident, particularly on the part of Petrograd textile workers, a contingent that was largely female and whose factories were still running.

Thus, on the surface at least, workers' protests seemed to be assuming a new and stronger political content, and one can readily understand in examining them why hopeful observers like Aronson became convinced that by June 1918 "a committed opposition . . . [had] gained the upper hand." Political values and affiliations seemed to lie at the heart of these protests; indeed, one can hardly deny their political character or import. Such protests, moreover, were not limited to Petrograd;[18] and in many places, elections to local soviets began to return large numbers of Menshevik and Socialist Revolutionary deputies, even majorities.[19]

[18] In Moscow, Tula, Iaroslavl', Briansk, and other places, gatherings like those in Petrograd took place in plants like the Tula armament works and the huge Sormovo complex in Nizhnii, formerly one of the country's major defense producers. In Moscow a gathering of more than four thousand railroaders in the Aleksandrovsk shops endorsed the conference's demand for civil liberties and an end to Bolshevik rule.

[19] See the discussion by Vladimir Brovkin, "The Mensheviks' Political Comeback." On elections to the Petrograd Soviet in July, which returned a comfortable Bolshevik majority, see David Mandel, *Petrograd Workers and the Soviet Seizure of Power*, 403–9.

On closer examination, the broader social dimensions of protest are also apparent, and in ways that suggest that social issues continued to be as important as politics, despite the political effect of almost every demonstration and work stoppage. As before, the overwhelming preponderance of protests came from displaced metalworkers. More than 75 percent of all incidents I have been able to catalog in Petrograd between the end of March and early July 1918 involved this group.

The largest number of incidents by far continued to center around such plants as the Patronnyi works and the Arsenal in the Vyborg district, the Obukhov works in the Nevskii district (where some 2,500 workers, with close ties in the past to the Socialist Revolutionaries, continued to struggle to fill state orders for locomotives), and Putilov — all of which had been devastated by the chaos of demobilization and evacuation. Only a handful of protests, largely short strikes over food rations, came from the city's textile plants, despite reports that workers here felt "things are worse now than under the tsar."

Although the evidence is incomplete, the patterns still seem evident. They correlate with what we have been able to surmise about the social composition of the conference delegates. Further corroborating evidence comes from the geographical distribution of the protests, which shows a heavy concentration in two districts — the Nevskii (Obukhov, Nevskii shipbuilding, and the Aleksandrovsk mechanical shops) and Vyborg (Arsenal, Old Lessner, the Old Baranovskii works, and the Patronnyi plant). There were also a number of protests in the Narvskii district, but on examination these seem almost entirely connected to Putilov. Other districts, including Vasil'evskii, were relatively quiet. Even in rough outline, this configuration reinforces the conclusion that protests came overwhelmingly from the ranks of displaced, semiskilled metalworkers who were, of course, geographically concentrated in the Nevskii and Vyborg districts.[20]

---

[20] We know, moreover, that residence patterns in the Vyborg district before 1918 had been relatively stable. This district, and to a lesser extent the Nevskii region, had a much smaller annual influx of migrants than the Vasil'evskii district and other outlying neighborhoods. While Vyborg district's population had increased over the past two decades, it also retained a large core of long-term, established city residents. Given the concentration of protests here in May and June 1918, it is reasonable to assume that the protesters were them-

Finally, we can also see further indication in these weeks of continued conflict between factory committee personnel and their rank and file; between higher paid skilled workers and their less well off, less skilled comrades, and, of course, between virtually everyone still struggling with the tasks of production at the factory level and those attempting to impose discipline from above. At Siemens-Schuckert and Obukhov, for example, there were incidents of violence as unemployed workers attempted to prevent others from entering the plant; at Putilov, shop committees openly refused to implement the directives of the factory committee and demanded a citywide meeting to discuss inequalities in wages. At a meeting of Vyborg district factory committees in mid-June, organized by the metalworkers' union, representatives stressed how negligent and hostile attitudes toward the committees greatly hindered production.

Throughout, strong anti-Bolshevik feelings remained evident. When meetings began in mid-June in connection with the Petrograd Soviet elections, in many plants prominent Bolsheviks had real difficulties making themselves heard.[21] But the importance of political commitments must be set in social context; the way the political drama was played out in Petrograd at the end of June makes clear that issues such as the Constituent Assembly and democratic government faded.

On June 20 V. Volodarskii, a popular and talented Bolshevik publicist and member of the Soviet Executive Committee, was killed on his way to an election meeting. This time reprisals were particularly swift. Large numbers of people were arrested, apparently including many workers. Again, angry meetings took place in factories around the city. At the Obukhov works a large delegation of sailors joined workers in issuing an appeal to the Conference of Factory and Plant Representatives to declare a one-day strike of protest on June 25. The Bolsheviks responded

selves largely long-term residents. Even though we lack direct evidence, this pattern is at least consistent with what we know about the evacuation during which the greatest number of departures were from the ranks of the unskilled and recent migrants. See James H. Bater, *St. Petersburg: Industrialization and Change* (London: Edward Arnold, 1976), esp. Chap. 4 and pp. 165–8, 250, 375.

[21] Zinoviev, Lunacharskii, and Volodarskii seem to have been treated with special rudeness, perhaps because they were all experienced and familiar orators whose style now angered their listeners.

by "invading" the whole Nevskii district with troops and shutting down Obukhov completely. Meetings everywhere were forbidden.[22]

This time, however, workers were not so readily pacified. In scores of additional factories and shops protests mounted and rapidly spread along the railroads. On the evening of June 26, the conference met in another "extraordinary session." Reports estimated that out of 146,000 workers still in Petrograd, as many as 100,000 supported the conference's goals. As a result, a general strike was declared for Tuesday July 2.

It is not really necessary to describe subsequent events in any detail, or to examine the organization and ultimate failure of the July 2 general strike. Zinoviev and others took quick counteraction, particularly on the railroads. Any sign of sympathy for the strike was declared a criminal act. More arrests were made. In Moscow, Bolsheviks raided the Aleksandrovsk railroad shops, not without bloodshed. Dissidence spread, particularly on the Nikolaev, Moscow-Kazan', and Moscow-Kursk railroads.

After meeting all night on June 28, the Council of People's Commissars issued its famous decree nationalizing all major branches of industry. As we know, the measure had long been contemplated, but resisted in part because it meant that the state would formally assume, at least indirectly, the responsibilities and unmanageable tasks of administration in nationalized plants. But it also meant, of course, a greater degree of state control. The irony was that the decree finally implemented what many workers had long demanded, even before October; but it was now the *party's* need for security, rather than the workers', that had become paramount. On July 1, as if to emphasize the point, machine guns were set up at main points throughout the Petrograd and Moscow railroad junctions, and elsewhere in both cities as well. Controls were tightened in factories. Meetings were forcefully dispersed.

All of this proved sufficient for Lenin's government to maintain order. When the morning of July 2 arrived, most trains were running. By evening it was clear that striking workers and the Conference of Factory and Plant Representatives both had failed,

[22] The Nevskii district was placed under "martial law," which, according to one report, produced an effect "like an exploding bomb."

and that proletarian Russia had reached another important turning point.

The end of proletarian independence

The events of late June signaled a crisis that extended through the assassinations of Mirbach and Uritskii, additional strikes, the attempt on Lenin's own life, and the unleashing in force of Red terror as the summer came to an end. Scores of additional arrests decimated the Conference of Factory and Plant Representatives. There was soon little question that the era of workers' control was over, supplanted now by the programs of War Communism and by a party dictatorship determined to enforce its own view of proletarian interests on recalcitrants everywhere.

Yet the history of proletarian Russia in the important first months of Bolshevik power indicates the weakness of seeing the consolidation of party rule in political terms alone, and the limits of explaining the workers' failure to maintain their own independence primarily in terms of Bolshevik repression. Without discounting the importance of force, one must recognize too that the failure of July 2 was evidence of Petrograd workers' inability to mobilize effectively in defense of their own self-defined interests and goals, as they had in 1917, particularly in Petrograd.

It is now possible to understand this failure, and to consider briefly what it suggests about the workers' movement and party–labor relations more broadly in the immediate post-October period. The first point to be emphasized is that in contrast to 1917 the promise of personal security and material betterment implicit in earlier labor activism was singularly absent in the spring of 1918; and unlike the Bolsheviks, neither the Conference of Factory and Plant Representatives nor other oppositional groups had either a compelling explanation for the new disasters besetting Russian workers, nor a clear and convincing vision of a viable alternative social order. The conference called for a general strike in the name of the Constituent Assembly, civil liberties, a single indivisible republic, and an end to repression, but these had little to do with solving the problems of food supply, unemployment, or production, or otherwise constructing an effective state economic apparatus. Indeed, the disaster was beyond short-term relief. This was true as well before October, and one might argue that the promises of 1917 were false and illusory. But they nonetheless had political force, whereas in the aftermath of October, no promises of betterment were persuasive.

Important here, in my judgment, is that workers themselves had largely completed the "expropriation" of Russia's bourgeoisie by the spring of 1918, and "capitalists" could no longer be identified as the primary cause of privation and want. Mobilization in the course of 1917 involved a discernible social enemy. Bolshevik strength grew not only because of the party's relative organizational strength, but also because of the explanatory content of party views and programs, and because workers were compelled by economic circumstances to organize both offensively and defensively against the "bourgeoisie." The complementary tasks of proletarian social and Bolshevik political revolution thus coalesced; so too did workers and party "professionals" in a period of increasing economic privation and social polarization, when Bolsheviks (and others) could provide most workers with seemingly clear ideas of an alternative, socialist, mode of production.

The destruction of Russia's "bourgeois order" complicated Lenin's own task of maintaining a high degree of political consciousness among workers after October, but it made those of the conference virtually impossible. The distinction drawn earlier between a Russian state and a bourgeois government no longer served to galvanize political resistance. Even as workers demonstrated against Bolshevik officials, the party remained a workers' party. Many voting in the soviet elections for Mensheviks and especially Left Socialist Revolutionaries were seeking, in effect, "better" Bolsheviks. Efforts to build a more politically democratic order thus had little foundation in the broader patterns of social dissidence; party politics themselves seemed irrelevant.

Even more important, and for reasons that should now be clear, the Petrograd labor movement in 1918 was very narrowly based in social terms. It may well have been, as delegates to conference meetings believed in late June, that the overwhelming majority of workers in the city "supported" conference goals. But those most active in the movement seem to have been preponderantly semiskilled metalworkers, who, despite their strong protests in the spring of 1918, had long been closely tied to the Bolsheviks.

Probably their political loyalties still lay in that direction. Their dissidence seems to have been directed more toward obtaining effective relief than in support of Mensheviks or other oppositional parties; and votes of protest are never the same as a commitment to the opposition. In any event, their concerns were primarily with issues of social security and well-being, something no political group could effectively meet in the first months after October.

Part of the opposition's difficulty also turned on problems associated with the workers' own local organizations, particularly factory committees. It is conceivable that in somewhat better economic circumstances, the Conference of Factory and Plant Representatives might have effectively allied with committee leaders in support of a more democratic political and economic administration. Yet not only were factory committees relatively powerless to protect worker interests in the spring of 1918; they clearly became themselves focal points of worker dissidence, partly as a result of hierarchy and social stratification within the workplace, partly because their tasks now were necessarily so onerous, especially in Petrograd metal plants. Paradoxically, proletarian dictatorship itself helped break elements of worker solidarity after October.

One can similarly understand from this perspective why even many opposition figures within the party had trouble accepting democratic organizations as an institutional basis for Bolshevik administration, and why many factory committees themselves came to repress democracy in their plants. The pressures for authority developed strongly, in other words, under conditions of labor conflict, particularism, and devastating economic privation. The deeper Russia's economic crisis, in fact, the more desperate the need for effective state control, something which in the end must have left even dissident metalworkers in Petrograd hoping that in the longer run Bolshevik power would still represent their interests.

In the spring and early summer of 1918 most Bolsheviks understood that conflicts among workers and the danger of anarchy posed real threats and jeopardized any socialist order whatsoever. Broader class consciousness and a muting of particularism also remained essential to any effective defense against the Whites and foreign intervention. In this respect the protests of May and June and the attempted general strike of July 2 may only have further impressed party leaders with the dangers of depoliticization and worker passivity, and the need to strengthen class consciousness as in 1917. These events also undoubtedly strengthened tendencies toward identifying and attacking "class enemies," and made new forms of repression more acceptable. In this sense, in the end, the ensuing civil war may have been as much an instrument of ultimate Bolshevik repression as it was simultaneously a danger and further threat; in any event, it marked as much the end of proletarian independence as the foundation of a new workers' state.

6

Conclusion: understanding the Russian Revolution

William G. Rosenberg
University of Michigan

If the views of so many American students about revolutions and revolutionary change were not still so firmly rooted in notions of political subversion and communist conspiracies, it would be less distressing (and distinctly less important) to urge a "rethinking" of 1917. Yet as the contributors to this volume have emphasized, Alexander Kerensky's view that "only by way of conspiracy, only by way of a treacherous armed struggle was it possible to break up the Provisional Government and stop the establishment of a democratic system . . ." is still broadly held; and similar arguments are frequently made about Nicaragua, Cuba, Vietnam, China, and other areas where social revolutions have helped propel Lenin's followers to power. Both the conceptual and factual weaknesses of this emphasis on subversion and conspiracy should now be apparent. So should the consequences in the contemporary world of perspectives and policies based on inadequate understanding of the relationships between political and social change. The complexities of such connections and the difficulties in perceiving them, sometimes offered after the fact as explanation of why things went wrong, only reinforce the need for serious, open-minded study, and the importance of asking ourselves what "wrong" means in revolutionary situations.

We need not dwell by way of conclusion on the factual weaknesses of the overemphasis on conspiratorial politics. As Professors Suny, Smith, and Koenker show very well, conspiracy explanations fail to appreciate both the development of social and institutional foundations of Bolshevik power in urban Russia,

132

and the corollary deterioration of the provisional regime's own institutional (or "infrastructural") base, ignoring in the process that Lenin came to power without significant resistance. And here it is not so much that Kerensky's last cabinet could not secure even 300 armed men to defend it, as the fact that Bolsheviks came to power through and for the notion of *soviet* rule – the idea, widely believed in October, that Russia's vast network of local and regional councils of workers, peasants, and soldiers, headed by a national congress of soviets and its executive committee, was better able to solve the crises of everyday political administration in revolutionary Russia than the self-appointed successors to the tsar. That they could not, for reasons I have partly suggested in my own contribution, was as much a shock and disappointment to many of Lenin's left-wing supporters as it was the basis for an enduring, repressive dictatorial regime.

What needs to be emphasized, rather, are the weaknesses in the ways many of us have *thought* about revolutionary Russia, and by extension, our conceptualization of revolutionary processes generally. And here, it seems to me, the contributions to this volume focus our attention on four central and closely connected issues: 1) the relationship between longer and shorter processes of social and political change; 2) the importance of social identity, class consciousness, and social polarization to the unfolding of events after February; 3) the relationship between political power and the superordinate authority of law in conditions of massive social dislocation and deprivation; and 4) the consequent meanings of "democracy" itself in such circumstances, as well as such closely related concepts as "legitimacy", "nation", and "national interest." Let us look briefly at each, recognizing in the process that the task of "rethinking" must be an ongoing one, extending far beyond the confines of this small volume.

Processes of social and political change

James Bater's contribution forces us to recognize the long-term demographic, social, and pathological consequences of rapid urban-centered industrialization in the last decades of the old regime, and to recognize that urban Russia on the eve of the first world war was in the throes of massive social dislocation that civil authorities found virtually impossible to resolve. The dismal conditions of working-class life in Moscow and St. Petersburg aroused conservatives and liberals alike, as a wide range of newspaper editorials testify; and the proximity of worker residences to those of the urban bourgeoisie could not help but foster a mutual and antagonistic awareness of the wide socioeconomic differentials tearing at Russia's social order. Whereas other European societies underwent comparable processes of modernization in these decades, a number of factors made Russia's experience especially severe, even in relative terms.

Most important were the conditions of the countryside and the marginal living standards of vast numbers of Russian peasants. This important aspect of Russia's social circumstances in the broad sense has not been addressed in this volume because of its lesser importance on the consolidation of urban-based Bolshevism. Rural Russia deeply affected events in the cities during 1917, of course, but even before, a continual influx of new industrial recruits from the countryside overwhelmed the efforts of well-intentioned municipal authorities to improve housing and sanitation conditions significantly, and contributed to what Bater and others have suggested was a virtually continuous administrative crisis. In addition to coping with the traumas of industrialization, the tasks of "modernization" in prerevolutionary Russia also meant lifting peasants and the rural economy as a whole from conditions of economic and social "backwardness," which, despite notable progress in this regard under Prime Minister Stolypin's stewardship, still taxed the tsarist regime to the hilt.

Yet modernization and urban industrialization were imperative if prerevolutionary Russia was to remain a viable and credible European power, and particularly if the country was to defend itself in an increasingly bellicose and competitive international order. Hence the long-term processes of change and dislocation meant that *any* state authorities, autocratic or otherwise, faced enormous and challenging problems even in conditions of peace and international stability, requiring the very best in administrative and political talent. With the outbreak of war, the shocking dearth of such talent in the tsar's regime mobilized conservatives and liberals alike in support of major reforms, complementing the growing pressures from below on the part of Moscow and Petrograd workers.

The shorter-term social, economic, and political dislocations of war vastly intensified these broader aspects of crisis in tsarist Russia and created the specific contours of the February revolutionary conjuncture. As Ronald Suny indicates, the overthrow of the tsar was the result of largely spontaneous action by tens of thousands of working men and women and garrison peasant-soldiers. But more important in some ways to what followed was the fact that the press of society's lower reaches was so extensively echoed above, from the legislative chambers of the State Duma to the councils of Petrograd and Moscow industrialists, all of whom railed at the tsarist regime's incompetence. Disaffection characterized *all* levels of society in February 1917; hence the rapidity and ease with which the old regime fell away.

Class consciousness and social polarization

But it soon became evident that this disaffection was of very different sorts, and that differences related directly to social identity. Since Imperial Russia was, of course, a society of carefully (and legally) defined estates, every one of the tsar's subjects was always aware of his or her social station, despite the increasing degree of mobility accompanying modernization. But the events of February made it clear that one's sense of what was wrong as well as one's perspectives on the country's social needs and national interest were largely contingent on where one stood in the social order. At the upper reaches of society the fundamental source of disaffection was the government's ineptitude in prosecuting the war. For many like the Provisional Government's new Foreign Minister, Paul Miliukov, the overthrow of the tsarist regime was both necessary and justified in terms of securing the military victory essential for the preservation of Russia's imperial interests. It was not simply that victory over Germany might bring Russia control over Constantinople and the Dardanelle straits, but that Russia would take its rightful place among the dominant powers of Europe, politically and economically. What

Russia required, in this view, was a government of able people and a vast improvement in the efficiency of both state and industrial administration, especially in defense production.

Miliukov and other liberal democrats of the first provisional cabinet believed the key to such efficiency – itself regarded as a central element to successful modernization – lay in part in the democratization of political and social relations. The idea here was certainly not the instant creation of representative government in the literal sense and even less the nationalization or socialization of private industry, but an end to the arbitrariness of autocratic practices and values wherever they affected public life. This view was shared by a surprising number of Moscow and Petrograd industrialists as well as other members of upper-level urban society who soon found themselves lumped together in the popular mind as Russia's "bourgeoisie." Middle-level managerial personnel in particular recognized the ways in which the arbitrariness of state and industrial administration had alienated workers and affected productivity so adversely. For these members of Russia's educated and largely liberal urban society, the new order was "representative" in the sense that it finally reflected the collective interests of all Russians. Democratic Russia meant that the state's interests genuinely reflected those of its people. In time – sooner at the level of local government, somewhat later at the level of state power – popular elections and representative institutions in the literal sense would make these linkages permanent.

Thus it was with the new government's support and encouragement that in March Petrograd manufacturers were able to reach a quick agreement with the city's industrial workers, one which involved, among other things, the creation of representative factory committees. Stability and order in the workplace seemed a central part of addressing the country's serious economic problems; and recognizing the workers' own committees seemed an important first step in securing harmonious labor-management relations. In April the government authorized similar committees for the country as a whole; and by May many of Russia's railroads were being guided by able groups of workers representing a number of different elements of the workforce, from engineers to shop workers, conductors, and engine drivers. Peasants in the countryside were similarly invited to participate in regional land committees, designed to address the manifold problems of agrarian productivity. Even in the army, soldiers' committees were recognized as having value in such matters as procuring supplies and otherwise assuring a unit's welfare. In sum, popular advice and consent was broadly regarded as both an appropriate and effective means for democratic Russia to address its problems, clearing the decks, as it were, for victory.

As the essays in this volume indicate so clearly, however, the importance of such worker (and peasant) institutions to Russia's revolutionary development in 1917 was not so much their efforts at resolving problems in the workplace (although as Steve Smith and Diane Koenker show so well, these efforts were far greater than much of the literature allows); their role in deepening working-class consciousness was even more important. Worker institutions helped identify the vibrant psychological attribute of social position with goals and interests at increasing variance with those of the bourgeoisie and the regime. The sources of antagonism were soon quite clear. Lockouts reflected a greater concern on the part of plant owners for profitability rather than workers' welfare; landlords defending their estates from seizure reflected a stronger commitment to property rights than new grain production; manufacturers unwilling to improve dismal housing or sanitation conditions, or reluctant to raise minimal wages seemed to reflect contempt for the very goals of material relief and social betterment that had brought Petrograd's workers into the streets in February.

That Russia's propertied classes should prove self-interested was hardly surprising, and certainly not what pressed urban workers increasingly toward Bolshevism. Rather, it was the inability of Russia's new state order to resolve these issues, and the growing belief that the government's values and goals as well as those of Russia's capitalists and bourgeoisie were fundamentally antagonistic to their own. Social polarization itself, in other words, long familiar in Russia, was less the issue than the identification of social position with particular forms of state power. The Provisional Government increasingly became for workers the instrument of the privileged; its institutions and values were "theirs." Soviet power was "ours"; and the idea of a soviet state became increasingly attractive as a means, finally, to satisfy popular needs.

Political power and the authority of law

Had urban Russia not found itself in the throes of deep-seated socioeconomic crisis in 1917, such a division might not in itself have moved Russia so quickly toward Bolshevism. The question, after all, was one of political hegemony on the part of one or another social group, characteristic (in some form) of all liberal democracies, and one can at least imagine the crystalization in conditions of peace and economic prosperity of broadly based opposing nationalist (liberal) and socialist coalitions, whose competition for power could be constitutionally regulated. The more recent example of Portugal is perhaps worth considering in this regard. The difficulty for revolutionary Russia, in other words, was not so much "dual power," as many believe, as what might clumsily be labeled "dual nonpower" – the inability, that is, of either set of political institutions to bring solutions to bear on Russia's deepening economic crisis and accompanying social unrest. The particular political configuration of Provisional Government cabinets was not so much the issue in this regard as the nature of power itself in 1917 and the ability of *any* cabinet to exercise it effectively.

It was particularly in these terms that Lenin's April Theses and the party's ensuing policies and strengthening organization grew increasingly important to the course of events. Lenin was able to identify clearly the relationships between different social and class interests and Russia's evolving political forms. He offered, as I have argued, both a persuasive explanation of why workers' interests were not being met in these conditions, and the promise in a Bolshevik-controlled soviet regime of a workable alternative. Both became central and crucial elements of worker consciousness in 1917 as a result, in large measure, of Bolshevik efforts; and without these perspectives, the evolution of the Provisional Government and of Russia itself would have been much different. Here as elsewhere in 1917, Lenin and his supporters played a determinant role.

Central to Lenin's explanation, moreover, although rarely if ever communicated to ordinary workers in these terms, was his association (following Marx) of the rule of law with the preservation of "bourgeois" social hegemony, and his similar (and closely related) identification of what the provisional regime termed "state" interests with the socioeconomic prerogatives of privileged rather than ordinary Russians. The efforts of liberal and socialist government leaders alike to establish a new political order in 1917 involved the herculean task of replacing the practices and values of autocracy with a rule of law. Such a transformation, involving a change in deep-rooted cultural and psychological orientations as well as day-to-day practical routines, is an enormously complex and difficult aspect of social change in the best of circumstances, and virtually impossible, unless supported by force, in conditions of scarcity and massive deprivation. In both urban and rural Russia throughout 1917, the right to property, the law of trespass, the sanctity of contract, the notion of tort, and even the concept of law in the legislative sense of the term all emerged as barriers to the immediate satisfaction of popular need. And insofar as government and soviet authorities both resorted frequently to fiat, as indeed the Western democracies themselves found it necessary to do in 1917, they unwittingly encouraged the very arbitrariness and authoritarianism they hoped to supplant. Diane Koenker is right on the mark, I think, when she shifts our focus from active Bolshevism to inactive state and civil authorities in explaining the Bolsheviks coming to power. But an essential aspect of this process was also the manner in which those attempting to exercise power before October could not invoke the "full power of the law" to implement change and satisfy need.

In such circumstances, it was hardly surprising that the legitimacy of Russia's new leadership itself in 1917 would soon come into question. As Paul Miliukov and other liberals themselves fully recognized, no one elected the provisional regime. It came to power when the leadership of the State Duma usurped, in effect, the tsar's authority in Petrograd, refusing to obey his order to disperse, and with only the barest of imperial sanctions through the pronouncement in which the Grand Duke Michael refused to take the throne. The legitimacy of the new order was founded, in effect, on its ostensible commitment to Russia's "national interest" on the one hand, and the sanctity of law as superordinate authority on the other, both purporting to transcend the particularistic interest of any class or group for the good of all Russians together. It was in this sense, above all, that the new order was democratic.

Such a "constitutional" base, of course, is fundamentally ethical in nature. Law transcends any one set of interests as a means of assuring "fairness" and "the equality of all before the law." The state and its interests transcend the wishes and needs of any one group of its citizens. In effect, law and the state both assume organic qualities, as if they exist – have a "life" – independently of and superior to individual human foundation, and hence are "worth dying for." As with any ethical system, consequently, Russia's new political structure depended fundamentally on the acceptance of these ideas by those whose well-being they were to protect and enhance.

Democracy and legitimacy

Students need not accept the Marxists' premise that such a bourgeois democracy emerges historically to facilitate and preserve capitalist socioeconomic relations to appreciate the ease with which Bolsheviks and others could make this argument in 1917. Given its inheritance, the provisional regime could not defend a rule of law without initially, at least, protecting privilege. Neither, in fact, could the leaders of the Soviet. And given Russia's place in a European state system in which *all* countries, including Russia's allies, struggled for the spoils of victory, it is difficult to imagine the tsar's successors promoting a conception of national welfare that was not tied in some way to bringing the war to successful conclusion – either without annexations and indemnities as the Soviet leadership demanded, or with rights to Constantinople and the Dardanelles, as Minister of Foreign Affairs Miliukov first insisted. Yet *both* courses, in effect, defended a bourgeois democratic state and hence protected the rights (and privileges) of Russia's social elites, at least for the time being.

What gave the Bolshevik movement such force in 1917, as the essays here so ably demonstrate, was that events and circumstances, not political philosophy, cultivated popular antagonism to a state system based on these values. Conditions themselves raised the question of whose interests the new legal order served, and what kind of social order would be enhanced by a successful completion of the war. And growing social conflict in the factories and elsewhere came increasingly to reflect a struggle over the very meaning of democracy and the proper nature of the Russian state. For increasing thousands of ordinary Russians, preserving democracy came to mean protecting and advancing their own well-being, and the very word soon came to represent not an ethically based constitutional system, but workers, peasants, soldiers, and *their* institutions exclusively. In these circumstances the most important components of Bolshevik ideology may well not have been Lenin's ideas on party organization or the seizure of the state, but his fundamental rejection of the ethical and moral premises of liberal democracy itself, premises to which many leading socialist moderates also subscribed. For Bolsheviks, law was not superordinate authority, but a tool of the privileged; the state was not an organic entity whose welfare superseded that of its constituent social parts, but simply an instrument through which a hegemonic social class exercised power. These concepts served *bourgeois* interests, *their* wealth, *their* war. The welfare of Russia's workers, peasants, and soldiers, like those of working people throughout the world, would only be served by a qualitatively different state and a radically new social system.

In order to understand Russia's revolutions of 1917, students must recognize, finally, that one's view of such powerful constructs as the "national interest" depend, ultimately, on whether one believes that social relations and political values protected by a particular state order should be preserved. Similarly, the question of whether one or another political group takes power legitimately depends on one's understanding of what "legitimacy" means, whether it reflects something like ethically based legal relationships and the attendant values of liberal democracy, or whether it means simply the ability of those in authority to use their power effectively to support the well-being of those they rule. The importance of 1917 as an object of study is, in part, that it brings these vital and transcendent issues to the fore; and however difficult the effort, students must continue to grapple with them and appreciate the significance of these issues if they wish to understand their own world, and give meaning to historical inquiry itself.

Suggestions for further reading

The Russian Revolution has generated an enormous literature, so the reader interested in finding more detail will have little difficulty locating additional titles. Most of these titles, however, concentrate upon the politics of the revolution, especially in Petrograd. The best of these make fascinating reading, even if they do leave out the perspective that the authors of the present book attempt to argue. Leon Trotsky's *History of the Russian Revolution* is available in many editions, and makes colorful reading. *Ten Days Which Shook the World,* John Reed's account of the October Revolution, is also widely available, and carries much of the excitement of the moment. Another observer's account that, if less dramatic, is nonetheless careful, is N. N. Sukhanov, *The Russian Revolution of 1917.* Many other participants in the Provisional Government have also published their reminiscences.

Since the sources for a social history of the revolution are often numeric or quite bulky, at present there is no handbook of materials to parallel those already published to illustrate the politics of the revolution. Nevertheless, readers can benefit from the following: Robert Browder and Alexander Kerensky, *The Russian Provisional Government, 1917. Documents,* 3 vols. (Stanford: Stanford University Press, 1961); James Bunyan, *Intervention, Civil War, and Communism in Russia (April–December 1918)* (Baltimore: Johns Hopkins University Press, 1936); James Bunyan and H. H. Fisher, *The Bolshevik Revolution 1917–1918: Documents and Materials* (Stanford: Stanford University Press, 1934); and Frank Golder, *Documents of Russian History 1914–1917* (New York: Century Company, 1927). Many other primary materials sur-

142

vive, but in the main they depict the revolution from the top.

In the secondary literature, too, politics dominates the narratives of the revolution. Nevertheless, readers interested in this perspective can read with profit William H. Chamberlin, *The Russian Revolution*, 2 vols. (New York: Grosset and Dunlap, 1965). Another classic account is E. H. Carr, *The Bolshevik Revolution, 1917–1923*, 3 vols. (New York: Macmillan, 1950–3). Typical of much Soviet writing on 1917 is *The Great October Socialist Revolution* (Moscow: Progress, 1977). Robert Daniels' book, *Red October: The Bolshevik Revolution of 1917* (New York: Charles Scribner's Sons, 1967), was very influential, and was reissued in 1984. Daniels argued that the Bolsheviks' organizational skills helped propel them through the social chaos of 1917, and almost accidentally they came to power. Among more recent works, similar interpretations appear in John L. H. Keep, *The Russian Revolution: A Study in Mass Mobilization* (New York: W. W. Norton, 1976), and Leonard B. Schapiro, *The Russian Revolutions of 1917; The Origins of Modern Communism* (New York: Basic Books, 1984).

For a criticism of some of these works, see Ronald Grigor Suny, "Toward a Social History of the October Revolution," *American Historical Review* 88(1983):31–52. The secondary literature that emphasizes social processes is not yet so voluminous, but the reader interested in worker perspectives might begin by reading some worker memoirs. Although confined to the period before 1905, the reminiscences of Semen Kanatchikov are very powerful (*A Radical Worker in Tsarist Russia: The Autobiography of Semën Kanatchikov*, ed., trans. Reginald E. Zelnik [Stanford: Stanford University Press, 1986]). Selections from Kanatchikov's and other workers' memoirs appear in *The Russian Worker: Life and Labor under the Tsarist Regime*, ed. Victoria E. Bonnell (Berkeley: University of California Press, 1983).

To sample the geographic and demographic context of the revolution, readers might consult Barbara Anderson, *Internal Migration During Modernization in Late Nineteenth-Century Russia* (Princeton: Princeton University Press, 1980); James H. Bater, *St. Petersburg: Industrialization and Change* (London: Edward Arnold, 1976); James H. Bater, "Some Dimensions of Urbanization and the Response of Municipal Government: Moscow and St. Petersburg," *Russian History*, 5, pt. 1 (1978): 46–63; James H. Bater, "The Industrialization of Moscow and St. Petersburg," in

Studies in Russian Historical Geography, eds. James H. Bater and R. A. French, 2 vols. (London: Academic Press, 1983), 2:279–303; and Barbara Evans Clements, "Working-Class and Peasant Women in the Russian Revolution, 1917–1923," *Signs* 8(1982):215–35.

One of the first works to emphasize the social background to the revolution was Leopold Haimson, "The Problem of Social Stability in Urban Russia, 1905–1917," *Slavic Review* 33(1964):619–42; ibid., 34(1965):1–22. Among more recent works that describe the early stages of proletarian politics are Victoria E. Bonnell, *Roots of Rebellion: Workers' Politics and Organizations in St. Petersburg and Moscow, 1900–1914* (Berkeley: University of California Press, 1983); Joseph Bradley, *Muzhik and Muscovite: Urbanization in Late Imperial Russia* (Berkeley: University of California Press, 1985); Rose L. Glickman, *Russian Factory Women: Workplace and Society, 1880–1914* (Berkeley: University of California Press, 1984); Heather Hogan, "Industrial Rationalization and the Roots of Labor Militance in the St. Petersburg Metalworking Industry, 1901–1914," *Russian Review* 42(1983):163–90; and Robert Johnson, *Peasant and Proletarian: The Working Class of Moscow in the Late Nineteenth Century* (New Brunswick: Rutgers University Press, 1979). Particularly helpful for setting the Moscow revolution in context is Laura Engelstein, *Moscow, 1905: Working-Class Organization and Political Conflict* (Stanford: Stanford University Press, 1982). *Slavic Review* (41[1982]:417–53) published several articles on labor violence in the nineteenth century, and these too merit attention. And Diane Koenker has examined the interplay between social and political life in working-class families in "Urban Families, Working-Class Youth Groups, and the 1917 Revolution in Moscow," in *The Family in Imperial Russia: New Lines of Historical Research,* ed. David L. Ransel (Urbana: University of Illinois Press, 1978), 280–304.

Other histories of the 1917 Revolution that emphasize social causes include: Marc Ferro, *The Russian Revolution of 1917* (London: Routledge and Kegan Paul, 1972); Marc Ferro, *October 1917: A Social History of the Russian Revolution* (London: Routledge and Kegan Paul, 1980); Tsuyoshi Hasegawa, *The February Revolution: Petrograd 1917* (Seattle: University of Washington Press, 1981); Diane Koenker, *Moscow Workers and the 1917 Revolution* (Princeton: Princeton University Press, 1981); David Mandel, *The Petro-grad Workers and the Fall of the Old Regime: From the February Rev-olution to the July Days, 1917* (London: Macmillan, 1983); David Mandel, *Petrograd Workers and the Soviet Seizure of Power (July 1917–June 1918)* (London: Macmillan, 1984); S. A. Smith, *Red Petro-grad: Revolution in the Factories 1917–1918* (Cambridge: Cam-bridge University Press, 1983).

Additional study of the factory committees appears in Paul H. Avrich, "Russian Factory Committees in 1917," *Jahrbücher für Geschichte Osteuropas* 11(1963):161–82; and Chris Goodey, "Fac-tory Committees and the Dictatorship of the Proletariat (1918)," *Critique* 3(Autumn 1974):27–47. Rex Wade has studied the local Petrograd soviets in "The Rajonnye Sovety of Petrograd: The Role of Local Political Bodies in the Russian Revolution," *Jahr-bücher für Geschichte Osteuropas* 20(1972):226–40; and Heather Hogan labor – management negotiation in "Conciliation Boards in Revolutionary Petrograd: Aspects of the Crisis of Labor–Management Relations in 1917," *Russian History* 9(1982):49–66.

Although primarily political, the works of Alexander Rabi-nowitch also attempt to revise the predominant estimate of Bolshevism and its role in the Russian Revolution. *Prelude to Revolution: The Petrograd Bolsheviks and the July 1917 Uprising* (Bloomington: Indiana University Press, 1968) and *The Bolshe-viks Come to Power: The Revolution of 1917 in Petrograd* (New York: W. W. Norton, 1976) both provide detailed examination of Bol-shevik politics and the response of the working class. The poli-tics of the center is detailed in William G. Rosenberg, *Liberals in the Russian Revolution: The Constitutional Democratic Party, 1917–1921* (Princeton: Princeton University Press, 1974). Vladimir Brovkin has examined the period after October in "The Men-sheviks' Political Comeback: The Elections to the Provincial City Soviets in Spring 1918," *Russian Review* 42(1983):1–50; and "The Mensheviks Under Attack: The Transformation of Soviet Poli-tics, June–September 1918," *Jahrbücher für Geschichte Osteuropas* 32(1984):378–91.

There is still not very much available in English on the revo-lution outside the capital cities. But the following titles, although for the most part devoted to politics, can be recommended: An-drew Ezergailis, *The 1917 Revolution in Latvia* (Boulder: East Eu-ropean Quarterly, 1974); Richard A. Pierce, "Toward Soviet

Power in Tashkent, February–October 1917," *Canadian Slavonic Papers* 17(1975):261–70; Donald J. Raleigh, *Revolution on the Volga: 1917 in Saratov* (Ithaca: Cornell University Press, 1985); Donald J. Raleigh, "Revolutionary Politics in Provincial Russia: The Tsaritsyn 'Republic' in 1917," *Slavic Review* 40(1981):194–209; Russell E. Snow, *The Bolsheviks in Siberia, 1917–1918* (London: Associated University Presses, 1977); Ronald Grigor Suny, *The Baku Commune, 1917–1918: Class and Nationality in the Russian Revolution* (Princeton: Princeton University Press, 1972); and Rex Wade, *Red Guards and Workers' Militias in the Russian Revolution* (Stanford: Stanford University Press, 1984).

Index